Mark Twain

Tom Sawyer *and* Huckleberry Finn

EDITED BY STUART HUTCHINSON

Series editor: Richard Beynon

COLUMBIA UNIVERSITY PRESS ◣◤ NEW YORK

Columbia University Press
Publishers Since 1893
New York   Chichester, West Sussex
Editor's text copyright © 1998 Stuart Hutchinson

First published in the Icon Critical Guides series in 1998
by Icon Books Ltd.

Library of Congress Cataloging-in-Publication Data

Mark Twain : Tom Sawyer/Huckleberry Finn / edited by Stuart
    Hutchinson.
        p.   cm. — (Columbia critical guides)
    Includes bibliographical references and index.
    ISBN 0–231–11540–7 (cloth : alk. paper). —
ISBN 0–231–11541–5 (pbk. : alk. paper)
    1. Twain, Mark, 1835–1910.   Adventures of Tom Sawyer.
2. Twain, Mark, 1835–1910.   Adventures of Huckleberry
Finn.   3. Adventure stories, American—History and criticism.
4. Mississippi River—In literature.   5. Boys in literature.
I. Hutchinson, Stuart.   II. Series.
PS1306.M37   1999
813'.4—dc21   98–39505

Printed in the United States of America

c 10 9 8 7 6 5 4 3 2 1
p 10 9 8 7 6 5 4 3 2 1

Contents

The immediate reception of *Tom Sawyer* in England and America and the question of how it relates to Twain's well established fame as a comic writer. William Dean Howells' association of its realism with 'charm'. Doubts about whether a book containing Injun Joe is suitable for children to read.

Twain's changes of direction as he wrote the novel and whether or not he ever achieved a coherent structure and a consistent central character. The novel's universal appeal, but also its appeal to a particular kind of American nostalgia. Tom as a portrait of the artist, and the relation of fantasy and realism in Twain. Whether the novel was censored by Twain's wife. The interdependence of Tom as hero and Injun Joe as villain. Injun Joe and racism in Twain. Twain and 'sappy women'.

When the various chapters were written between the starting date, July 1876, and the completion slightly more than seven years later. The crucial abandoning of the novel at the end of chapter 16. The reception of the novel in America and Twain's own responsibility for having relatively few review copies sent out. The Concord Library ban and other incidents ensuring controversial publicity for the novel. Recognition of Twain as 'a literary artist of very high order', but immediate doubts about the novel's ending.

Mark Twain's Life and Work

■ EMERSON, LONGFELLOW, Lowell, Holmes – I knew them all and all the rest of our sages, poets, seers, critics, humorists; they were like one another and like other literary men; but Clemens was sole, incomparable, the Lincoln of our literature. □
William Dean Howells, *My Mark Twain*, 1, New York, London 1910, (Ch.26)

The Samuel Langhorne Clemens remembered by his friend Howells was born 30 November 1835 in Florida, Missouri, the third of the five children of John Marshall Clemens and Jane Lampton. When he was four his family moved to the slightly bigger Hannibal, Missouri, the burgeoning town (population 450) on the banks of the Mississippi which, in various guises, was to become the St Petersburg of *Tom Sawyer* (1876), the towns in *Huckleberry Finn* (1884–85), the Dawson's Landing of *Pudd'nhead Wilson* (1894), and even the Eseldorf of *The Mysterious Stranger* (1916). His father had inherited three slaves and, since he had studied law and had a claim on property in Tennessee, considered himself a member of the professional classes. His unrealistic ambitions, which never achieved financial security for the family, are gently satirised in the character Squire Hawkins in *The Gilded Age* (1873). He died in March 1847, leaving the 11 years old Clemens to make his own way by working for his older brother, Orion, as a printer, an occupation he followed in Hannibal till he was seventeen. He was already writing and on 1 May 1852 'The Dandy, Frightening the Squatter' appeared in *The Carpet Bag*, a weekly humorous magazine published in Boston. The years 1853–57 were a period of travel, with Clemens sustaining himself as a printer and contributor to newspapers in St Louis, Philadelphia, Muscatine and Keokuk (Iowa), and Cincinnati. Then he planned a trip to make his fortune in South America, only to get diverted into becoming a pilot on Mississippi steamboats. His writing continued and three humorous accounts of his activities were published in the *Keokuk Saturday Post* under the name Thomas Jefferson Snodgrass. More famously, these years were also to provide the material for 'Old Times on the Mississippi' (1875), in which learning to be a pilot on the mighty river becomes a humorous auto-biographical account of innocence developing into experience.

In 1858 Clemens' brother, Henry, was killed in a steamboat explosion. Two years later river traffic was disrupted by the Civil War. Clemens volunteered for the Missouri militia and fought for a few uncertain weeks on the Confederate side. Not till 1885, in 'The Private History of a Campaign that Failed' did he attempt to get a perspective on these weeks. In this anti-war piece the narrator again sets himself up as rather innocent and foolish, but the triumph of the humour is that many of us would rather be foolish with him than sensible with those who are killing and getting killed. At the heart of the story, as at the heart of *Huckleberry Finn*, is the consciousness of inescapable guilt integral with the consciousness of inescapable death. The Civil War, Clemens decided, was not his fight. In 1861 he accompanied Orion to the Nevada Territory, where Orion had a job as Secretary to the territorial government, and where Clemens again hoped to make his fortune, this time in the silver-mine bonanza. *Roughing It* (1872) records this western experience (1861–66), during which Clemens was a miner and prospector in Nevada, a reporter and free-lance writer for the Virginia City *Territorial Enterprise* and for San Francisco newspapers, and eventually a correspondent from Hawaii for the *Sacramento Union*. In December 1863 he met briefly the humorous lecturer Artemus Ward (Charles Farrar Browne), who was on a tour of the far West, and shortly afterwards Bret Harte. About this time he adopted the name 'Mark Twain'. 'Jim Smiley's Jumping Frog', which marked the beginning of his national fame, was intended for inclusion in *Artemus Ward: His Travels* (1865), but it arrived too late in New York. Instead it was published in the *New York Saturday Press* 18 November 1865 and then immediately circulated in newspapers throughout the country. A wonderfully funny tall-tale, having two narrators, the first using formal English, the second western slang, it initiates the complications of Twain's perspectives on the West and the East later developed in *Roughing It*.

On his return to San Francisco from Hawaii, Twain began his career as a lecturer, reporting on his recent trip. He was increasing his expertise in controlling audiences and timing jokes, especially in oral narrative. He was soon on the move again, sailing for New York, in December 1866, as correspondent for the San Francisco *Alta California*. He visited St Louis, Hannibal and Keokuk in Spring 1867, and May of this year saw the pub-lication of *The Celebrated Jumping Frog of Calaveras County and Other Sketches*. Now he persuaded the *Alta California* and the *New York Tribune* to finance him as their correspondent on the *Quaker City* voyage (June–November 1867) to Europe and the Holy Land. This experience became *The Innocents Abroad* (1869), an enormously popular and funny book, and a seminal account of an American encounter with the Old World. Like Huck Finn later, one of the Mark Twains in this book 'don't take no stock in dead people'. The Old World and its pretensions can be ridiculed, and the New World need not feel inferior. Other Mark Twains, however, are overwhelmed (at Versailles, for example) by the splendours of the past. Perhaps it has already pre-empted the future, its failures being ominous for New World hopes. America's response might amount only to flaunting its emerging material power and seizing souvenirs. Already in *The Innocents Abroad* the torments of American imperialism, seen in *A Connecticut Yankee* (1889) and Twain's later essays, are looming.

Back in New York Twain was introduced to Olivia Louise Langdon ('Livy'), the sister of Charles Jervis Langdon who had been on the *Quaker City* voyage, and the daughter of a wealthy coal magnate in Elmira, New York. They were married in February 1870, and a son, Langdon, was born in November, the family settling in Hartford, Connecticut in 1871. The following year their daughter Susan was born, but Langdon died later that year. *Roughing It* was published in 1871, its account of the western New World being as varied and complex as the engagement with the Old World in *The Innocents Abroad*. Twain wrote nothing again as exhilarating and liberating as its first twenty chapters, recalling the journey by stagecoach to Carson City, Nevada. There he participates as a miner in the feverish hunt for a fortune. Nothing else, it seems, motivates the New World, and there is an underlying sense of futility. Already there are ghost mining towns, cities of the dead recalling Pompeii. Only the narrator's humour and the ability always to move on keep him going.

There were lecture tours in England in 1872 and 1873. Meanwhile *The Gilded Age,* co-written with Charles Dudley Warner, focused mainly on the scams of the post-Civil War period. It has effective political satire and evocative pre-Civil War scenes in the barely developed territory of Twain's childhood, but it also demonstrates how little creative energy Twain has for a novel of manners involving plot and the consistent development of characters. In 1874 another daughter, Clara, was born, and the Clemenses built a mansion in Hartford, where they began to entertain lavishly. Twain had met William Dean Howells in 1869, and 'Old Times on the Mississippi', was serialised in the prestigious *Atlantic Monthly,* now edited by Howells. *The Adventures of Tom Sawyer* followed a year later in 1876, and December 1877 saw the occasion of the 'Whittier Birthday Speech' in Boston, when Twain apparently embarrassed his audience and then felt mortified himself as a result of his very funny mockery of Emerson, Longfellow and Holmes. During 1878–79 there were extended visits to Germany, Switzerland and Italy which furnished material for the comparatively weak and aimless *A Tramp Abroad* (1880). By now Twain had begun his eventually ruinous speculation in the Paige typesetter. In *The Prince and the Pauper* (1882), a historical romance, the theme of identity switching anticipated its more challenging black/white treatment in *Pudd'nhead Wilson* (1894). Off and on he had been writing *Huckleberry Finn* since 1876, but he turned to it again on re-acquainting himself with the Mississippi River as he expanded 'Old Times on the Mississippi' into *Life on the Mississippi* (1883). Arguably, a reading tour with George Washington Cable, who was a campaigner for rights for blacks, also influenced Twain's return to the writing of what was to become his greatest novel.

Yale gave Twain an honorary M.A. in 1888, and *A Connecticut Yankee* was published in 1889. Conflicting energies break through into this novel, hardly allowing it to achieve itself. It is aggressively nationalistic on behalf of American material and political achievement, and yet racked with the apparent vulgarity and soullessness of this enterprise. In an ominous allegory for the twentieth century, King Arthur's kingdom, which might represent any apparently primitive society, is derided and humiliated by the modern Yankee, who can command an arsenal of smart weaponry to enforce his version of life. Twain, for his part, settled in the Old World during 1891–95, living in Germany, Italy and France. 'A Whisper to the Reader', which prefaces *Pudd'nhead Wilson,* is written from Florence, as Twain tries to reconcile himself to Old World and New and indulge in remembrance of the riverbank town of his boyhood, only to be reminded yet again that slavery was at the heart of the whole system. Meanwhile the Paige typesetter was pronounced a failure in 1894 and Twain's own publishing company went bankrupt. Vast amounts of his own money and Livy's were lost, and in 1895–96 Twain embarked on a round-the-world lecture tour to repay his debts. He visited the Pacific Northwest, Australia, New Zealand, Ceylon, India, and South Africa. *Following the Equator* (1897) was one of the results, an essential book for understanding Twain's final positions on race and imperialism. *Personal Recollections of Joan of Arc* (1896) had illustrated, by contrast, all his sentimental desire to escape complication. Joan is a heroine of incorruptible virtue, an untwisted Huck Finn who can guarantee to do right without any of his wrong thoughts.

Having lived in Vienna and London for three years, Twain was back in New York in 1900, joining Howells in the anti-imperialism campaign but remaining on intimate terms with the leaders of big business. The increasingly cynical cast of his mind is expressed in the title story of *The Man that Corrupted Hadleyburg and Other Stories* (1900). By 1903 he was again in Florence on account of Livy's health, but she died there on 5 June 1904. Oxford gave Twain a Litt.D. in 1907. He built a new house, 'Stormfield' near Redding, Connecticut in 1908, and there on 21 April 1910 he too died. *The Mysterious Stranger* was published in 1916. It affirmed the surrender to determinism and despair also expressed in

What is Man? and Other Essays (1917). To its central character, the laughter which had had a claim on joy and liberation up to *Huckleberry Finn* and beyond, is now no more than a 'weapon'; its proponent, 'a vagrant thought, a useless thought, a homeless thought, wandering forlorn among the empty eternities'.

CHAPTER ONE

The Adventures of Tom Sawyer (1876): The Contemporary Reviews

TOM SAWYER was published in England in June 1876, nearly six months before it appeared in the United States. Nearly forty years after Ralph Waldo Emerson's declaration of American cultural independence in 'The American Scholar' ('our long apprenticeship to the learning of other lands draws to a close. . . . We have listened too long to the courtly muses of Europe'), even a writer from the banks of the Mississippi was still implicated in the expectations and machinery of an older culture. So the reviewer in the *Athenaeum* concludes by suggesting that it would have been as well if the author of *Tom Sawyer* had written more uniformly in English! He begins, however, by affirming Twain's fame as a comic writer:

■ The name of Mark Twain is known throughout the length and breadth of England. Wherever there is a railway-station with a book-stall his jokes are household words. Those whose usual range in literature does not extend beyond the sporting newspapers, the *Racing Calendar* and the *Diseases of Dogs,* have allowed him a place with Artemus Ward alongside of the handful of books which forms their library. For ourselves, we cannot dissociate him from the railway-station, and his jokes always rise in our mind with a background of Brown & Polson's Corn Flour and Taylor's system of removing furniture. We have read *The Adventures of Tom Sawyer* with different surroundings, and still have been made to laugh; and that ought to be taken as high praise. Indeed, the earlier part of the book is, to our thinking, the most amusing thing Mark Twain has written. The humour is not always uproarious but it is always genuine and some-times almost pathetic, and it is only now and then that the heartiness of a laugh is spoilt by one of those pieces of self-consciousness which are such common blots on Mark Twain's other books.[1] □

'[J]okes', 'jokes', 'made to laugh'; is it enough to see Twain entirely as a comic writer who is fittingly to be associated with Artemus Ward, the pen-name of Charles Farrar Browne (1834–67)? Twain knew Ward briefly in California and Nevada during December 1863, and he and Ward became the two most famous mid-nineteenth century American humorists. The tall-tale, dialect, deadpan manner, malapropisms and misspellings were the common resources of both writers, as they were of frontier humour generally. These are exploited by Twain in 'The Celebrated Jumping Frog of Calaveras County' which under its original title ('Jim Smiley's Jumping Frog') was intended for publication in *Artemus Ward: His Travels* (1865), but arrived too late for inclusion. An initial line of inquiry into Twain might ask how far beyond these roots he reached. The above reviewer points to 'those pieces of self-consciousness which are such common blots'. No examples are given, but in *Tom Sawyer* they might be such moments as the description of the storm in chapter 17, or the reflection on Injun Joe's death in chapter 34. The first of these can be contrasted to its disadvantage with Huck's account of the storm in chapter 9 of *Huckleberry Finn*. In the later book Samuel Clemens, who like Tom Sawyer always needed to release himself in a performing identity, can escape self-consciousness in a double disguise. He is Mark Twain and then Huck Finn. In *Tom Sawyer* he is only Mark Twain, primarily famous for humour.

The *Athenaeum* continues:

■ *The Adventures of Tom Sawyer* is an attempt in a new direction. It is consecutive, and much longer than the former books, and as it is not put forward as a mere collection of *Screamers,* we laugh more easily, and find some relief in being able to relax the conventional grin expected from the reader of the little volumes of railway humour. The present book is not, and does not pretend to be a novel, in the ordinary sense of the word; it is not even a story, for that presupposes a climax and a finish; nor is it a mere boys' book of adventures. In the Preface the author says, 'Although my book is intended mainly for the entertainment of boys and girls, I hope it will not be shunned by men and women on that account, for part of my plan has been to try pleasantly to remind adults of what they once were themselves, and of how they felt and thought and talked, and what queer enterprises they sometimes engaged in.' Questions of intention are always difficult to decide. The book will amuse grown-up people in the way that humorous books written for children have amused before, but (perhaps fortunately) it does not seem to us calculated to carry out the intention here expressed. With regard to the style, of course there are plenty of slang words and racy expressions, which are quite in place in the conversations, but it is just a question whether it would not have been as well if the remainder of the book had not been written more uniformly in English. □

Questions of form and structure, always tricky in Twain, are raised here. As a matter of fact *Tom Sawyer* is not longer than *The Innocents Abroad* (1869) or *Roughing It* (1872); nor is it longer than *The Gilded Age* (1873), the novel Twain co-wrote with Charles Dudley Warner. The first two of these do not pretend to be novels, but they are consecutive journey narratives in an autobiographical form, and they have some recurrent characters. They are adventures of Mark Twain created from the experience of Samuel Clemens. *The Gilded Age,* which has given its name to the post-Civil War period of American history, is more conventionally a novel of plot and character, but no-one would acclaim it on these grounds. When Twain writes *Tom Sawyer,* therefore, he is making a single-handed attempt at something he has not done before: the consistent development of a central character, relating to other characters, and all of them in defined personal and social circumstances in an established and constant location. Despite the *Athenaeum,* the result is a novel, but, as we shall see, questions about the sureness of Twain's achievement and about his intention still persist. As for the suggestion that an American author writes 'more uniformly in English', it reminds us what a crucial issue language was for nineteenth century American writers. With emerging American language to draw on, they had resources unknown to their British counterparts. They had resistances to their inheritance of British literature. Its plots, as Tom Sawyer was to discover, did not always work on the banks of the Mississippi.

The following review by William Dean Howells was well in advance of *Tom Sawyer*'s appearance in the States, an occurrence which amused Twain. Howells had been his friend since 1869 and was to remain his lifelong friend. He edited the enormously influential and prestigious *Atlantic Monthly* which in 1875 had serialised Twain's 'Old Times on the Mississippi', referred to in the review as the 'piloting reminiscences'. Howells had seen *Tom Sawyer* in manuscript and given his advice about the novel. Notice he refers to 'Clemens', thus indicating the distinction between the man from whose experience the work originates and his performing identity as author:

■ Mr Clemens . . . has taken the boy of the Southwest for the hero of his new book and has presented him with a fidelity to circumstance which loses no charm by being realistic in the highest degree, and which gives incomparably the best picture of life in that region as yet known to fiction. The town where Tom Sawyer was born and brought up is some such idle, shabby little Mississippi River town as Mr Clemens has so well described in his piloting reminiscences, but Tom belongs to the better sort of people in it, and has been bred to fear God and dread the Sunday-school according to the strictest rite of the faiths that have characterised all the respectability of the West. His subjection in these respects does not so deeply affect his inherent tendencies but that he makes himself a beloved burden to the poor, tender-hearted old aunt who brings him up with his orphan brother and sister, and struggles vainly with his manifold sins, actual and imaginary. The limitations of his transgressions are nicely and artistically traced. He is mischievous, but not vicious; he is ready for almost any depredation that involves the danger and honour of adventure, but profanity he knows may provoke a thunderbolt upon the heart of the blasphemer, and he almost never swears; he resorts to any stratagem to keep out of school, but he is not a downright liar, except upon terms of after shame and remorse that make his falsehood bitter to him. He is cruel, as all children are, but chiefly because he is ignorant; he is not mean, but there are very definite bounds to his generosity; and his courage is the Indian sort, full of prudence and mindful of retreat as one of the conditions of prolonged hostilities. In a word, he is a boy, and merely, and exactly an ordinary boy on the moral side. What makes him delightful to the reader is that on the imaginative side he is very much more, and though every boy has wild and fantastic dreams, this boy cannot rest till he has somehow realised them.[2] □

During the 1880s Howells, himself a significant novelist, was to become a powerful champion of realism, a quality he admires in *Tom Sawyer*. He does not find in it, however, the more challenging realism of Zola or Stephen Crane, novelists whom he was also to promote. Its realism is associated with 'charm', a word which catches a good deal of the intention expressed in the novel's Preface. Tom belongs to 'the better sort of people' and his community embodies all 'the respectability of the West'. He has been 'bred to fear God and dread the Sunday-school'. This last comment alerts us to the importance of religion, especially its Calvinist versions, in Twain. Howells does not develop his point, but 'fear' might warn us that religion does not bring happiness to Twain's central figures. Rather it is associated with the burden of conscience and guilt. In his generosity towards *Tom Sawyer* Howells also wants to reassure readers. Tom 'is mischievous, but not vicious'. True, yet Twain has sufficient sense of the character's possibilities, and of possibilities within himself, to write in chapter 19 of 'all the vicious vanity that was in him'. Later, according to Justin Kaplan,[3] he was to disparage Theodore Roosevelt as 'the Tom Sawyer of the political world of the 20thC'. Howells finds nothing to disturb him in Tom Sawyer. The novel contains Injun Joe, but Howells can use the term 'Indian' unproblematically. None the less he provides a key in finding Tom 'ordinary' on the moral side, but 'on the imaginative side . . . very much more [than ordinary]'.

Howells continues:

■ The local material and the incidents with which his career is worked up are excellent, and throughout there is scrupulous regard for the boy's point of view in reference to his surroundings and himself, which shows how rapidly Mr Clemens has grown as an artist. We do not remember anything in which this propriety is violated, and its preservation adds immensely to the grown-up reader's satisfaction in the amusing and exciting story. There is a boy's love-affair, but it is never treated otherwise than as a boy's love-affair. When the half-breed has murdered the young doctor, Tom and his friend, Huckleberry Finn, are really, in their boyish terror and superstition, going to let the poor old town-drunkard be hanged for the crime till the terror of that becomes unendurable. The story is a wonderful study of the boy-mind, which inhabits a world quite distinct from that in which he is bodily present with his elders, and in this lies its great charm and its universality for boy nature, however human nature varies, is the same everywhere.

The tale is very dramatically wrought, and the subordinate characters are treated with the same graphic force that sets Tom alive before us. The worthless vagabond, Huck Finn, is entirely delightful throughout, and in his promised reform his identity is respected: he will lead a decent life in order that he may, one day, be thought worthy to become a member of that gang of robbers which Tom is to organize. Tom's aunt is excellent, with her kind heart's sorrow and secret pride in Tom; and so is his sister Mary, one of those good girls who are born to usefulness and charity and forbearance and unvarying rectitude. Many village people and local notables are introduced in well-concealed character; the whole little town lives in the reader's sense, with its religiousness, its lawlessness, its droll social distinctions, its civilisation qualified by its slaveholding, and its traditions of the wilder West which has passed away. The picture will be instructive to those who have fancied the whole Southwest a sort of vast Pike County, and have not conceived of a sober and serious and orderly contrast to the sort of life that has come to represent the Southwest in literature. Mr William M Baker gives a notion of this in his stories, and Mr Clemens has again enforced the fact here in a book full of entertaining character and of the greatest artistic sincerity. □

Later critics will not be as confident as Howells about the consistency of Twain's 'scrupulous regard for the boy's point of view'. Perhaps the need to make this claim results from discussions Howells had been having with Henry James about the novelist's craft. Other qualities he finds in *Tom Sawyer,* however, are irrefutable, though we may always want to dig deeper, for example, about the slaveholding.

The last review to be referred to concerns itself with the everlasting question of what it is suitable for children to read. Interrelated is the patriotic question of the qualities the American nation needs to breed in its young men: 'courage, frankness, truthfulness, and self-reliance are to be inculcated in our lads'. The review alerts us to a range of reader demands any novel may be asked to satisfy, whether or not it wants to:

■ We have before expressed the idea that a truly clever child's book is one in which both the man and the boy can find pleasure. No child's book can be perfectly acceptable otherwise. Is *Tom Sawyer* amusing? It is incomparably so. It is the story of a Western boy, born and bred on the banks of one of the big rivers, and there is exactly, that wild village life which has schooled many a man to self-reliance and energy. Mr Clemens has a remarkable memory for those peculiarities of American boy-talk which the grown man may have forgotten, but which return to him not unpleasantly when once the proper key is sounded. There is one scene of a quarrel, with a dialogue, between Tom and a city boy which is perfect of its kind. Certain chapters in Tom's life, where his love for the schoolgirls is told, make us believe that for an urchin who had just lost his milk-teeth the affections out West have an awakening even earlier than in Oriental climes. In fact, Tom is a preternaturally precocious urchin.[4] □

How heterogeneous are the audiences American literature must contend with as it establishes itself! In the States there is an audience in the East, where the review is published, and one 'out West'. Later, the reviewer speaks of Twain's English readers, but also says Twain's sense of fun is 'of the true American kind'. What is meant by this last comment is not defined, but the assertion invites an exploration of whether Twain's humour is uniquely and typically American. Might we conclude that it is American in the sense that it functions entirely on behalf of itself and is never in aid of anything, so that Twain would eventually face despair when the jokes no longer provided relief? For the rest, the above reviewer would clearly not agree with Howells about the consistency of the presentation of Tom as a boy. The character does seem at least a youth in some of the scenes with Becky. Finally, the review returns to its moral concerns:

■ In the books to be placed into children's hands for the purposes of recreation, we have preference for those of a milder type than *Tom Sawyer. . . .* A sprinkling of salt in mental food is both natural and wholesome; any cravings for the contents of the castors, the cayenne and mustard, by children, should not be gratified. With less, then, of Injun Joe and 'revenge', and 'slitting women's ears', and the shadow of the gallows, which throws an unnecessary sinister tinge over the story, (if the book really is intended for boys and girls) we should have liked *Tom Sawyer* better. □

As the last sentence demonstrates, this reviewer has been engaged by ingredients ignored by the previous two and fascinating to modern readers.

CHAPTER TWO

Tom Sawyer: Twentieth Century Criticism

HOWELLS MUST have known about Twain's changes of direction in *Tom Sawyer*, even though his review makes nothing of the changes, nor of the structural problems in the published novel. Modern criticism has focused on these changes as part of its discussion of Twain's methods of composition, and of his ability to achieve a sense of unity and development in any one of his works. Hamlin L. Hill[1] debates these issues and points to a 'divergence among Twain scholars':

■ Walter Blair's study 'On the Structure of *Tom Sawyer*'[2] suggested that the book was organised as the story of a boy's maturation, presented to the reader through four lines of action – the Tom and Becky story, the Muff Potter story, the Jackson's Island adventure, and the Injun Joe story – each of which begins with an immature act and ends with a relatively mature act by Tom. □

Hill cites numerous critics who support or refute Blair. Among the latter is DeLancey Ferguson who argues that '*Tom Sawyer*, . . . grew as grows the grass; it was not art at all, but it was life'.[3]

According to Hill, Twain

■ began work on *Tom Sawyer* itself, as distinguished from its several precursors,[4] probably in the summer of 1874. By September 4th he 'had worked myself out, pumped myself dry,'[5] so he put the manuscript aside until the spring or summer of 1875, and on July 5th 1875, announced its completion.[6] Years later, he described the crisis which presumably came in September 1874:

At page 400 of my manuscript the story made a sudden and determined halt and refused to proceed another step. Day after day it still refused. I was not finished and I could not understand why I was not able to go on with it. The reason was very simple – my tank had run dry; it was empty; the stock of materials in it was exhausted; the story, could not go on without materials; it could not be wrought out of nothing.[7]

And Brander Matthews, reporting a discussion with Twain, confirmed this haphazard method of composition:

He began the composition of *Tom Sawyer* with certain of his boyish recollections in mind, writing on and on until he had utilized them all, whereupon he put his manuscript aside and ceased to think about it, except in so far as he might recall from time to time, and more or less unconsciously other recollections of those early days. Sooner or later he would return to his work and make use of memories he had recaptured in the interval.[8]

The manuscript provides many examples of this plot development through recollection and association.

While writing or reading over the early parts of *Tom Sawyer* Twain apparently remembered ideas and incidents from his earlier writings or his own boyhood which he felt might be of use to him later. Accordingly, he wrote notes and suggestions in the margins of his manuscript, mentioning material which would either be utilized later in the book or be discarded.[9] □

The above quotation from Twain himself might apply to the composition of any of his longer works. As Hill sees it, all the above evidence together with much else he cites,

■ supports the theory that *Tom Sawyer* was structureless. The author's own statements suggested that he wrote those memories of his childhood which came to mind, waited until he remembered some more, and then added them to his manuscript. The marginal notations show that as he wrote he thought of other incidents by association and made his notes to keep them in mind. In one instance the associative link between the material he was writing and the marginal note is apparent. On page 209 he was describing Tom Sawyer's daydream of returning to St Petersburg as a pirate wearing a 'crimson sash.' A red sash was the enticement which the author could not resist as a boy, when joining the Cadets of Temperance, and, remembering this, he wrote the 'Cadets of Temp.' note in his margin. This was sheer opportunism, but it was the way he collected the material for the book – from immediate memory and from brief notes in his margins which he would later expand.[10] □

But now Hill finds support for Blair's position:

■ . . . it occurs on the first page of the manuscript. Here Twain wrote a long note, never before discussed, which merits careful study:

> 1 Boyhood & youth; 2 y. & early manhood; 3 the Battle of Life in many lands; 4 (age 37 to [40?]) return & meet grown babies & toothless old drivelers who were the grandees of his boyhood. The Adored Unknown a [illegible] faded old maid & full of rasping, puritanical vinegar piety.

This outline was written, if not before he began the book, before he reached page 160 of his manuscript. Before that page, the 'new girl' was referred to as 'the Adored Unknown' (chapter 11 of the published book). And on that page the name 'Becky Thatcher' appeared for the first time (chapter VI). If Becky had been 'christened' when Twain wrote this outline, it seems likely that he would have used her name in it. The marginal note represents, then, a very early, if not the earliest plan for the plot of the new novel. The book was to be in four parts, clearly progressing from boyhood to maturity and ending with Tom's return to St Petersburg and a puritanical Becky. The 'return' idea was a recurrent one, appearing in Twain's notebooks several times.[11] Rudimentary though it is, this outline assumes enormous importance, for the only 'theme' it conveys is one of the maturation of a person from boyhood to manhood. It is obviously critical to determine exactly when this plan was discarded, because if Twain composed the book by this formula the 'maturation' theory stands vindicated.

Even after the book was finished, Twain was uncertain about the wisdom of having stopped with Tom's youth. 'I have finished the story and can't take the chap beyond boyhood,' he told Howells. 'See if you don't really decide that I am right in closing with him as a boy.'[12] But, the decision to alter the original outline was not made until after September 4th 1874, and perhaps as late as the spring of 1875.

Page 403 of the manuscript, where the change is noticeable, appears toward the end of chapter XV. Tom, Joe Harper and Huck have run away to Jackson's Island to become pirates. Joe and Huck, homesick and ready to return to St Petersburg, have been 'withered with derision' by Tom, who has no desire to go back to civilisation. The cannons of the ferry boat have failed to bring up the boys' bodies. Just as in *Huckleberry Finn,* the stage has been set, the devices prepared, for an imminent departure. After the other boys go to sleep, Tom scrawls a note to Joe Harper on a piece of sycamore bark and leaves it, together with his 'schoolboy treasures of almost inestimable value.' This leave-taking from Joe thus sounds much more final than would be necessary merely for Tom to deliver a note to his Aunt. Tom writes another note for Aunt Polly, returns to his home in St Petersburg, and at page 403 is standing over his sleeping aunt.

Preparations were thus made for Tom to begin his 'Battle of Life in many Lands' to leave both St Petersburg and his comrades who were about to return there. But Mark Twain's manuscript shows that he pondered the wisdom of having Tom depart. Aware that a critical point in the story was at hand, he sprinkled the page with signs of his indecision. Deliberating what course to take, he wrote at the top margin 'Sid is to find and steal that scroll,' and 'He is to show the scroll in proof of his intent.' In the left margin, he wrote two further lines and cancelled them. Across the page itself he wrote, 'No, he leaves the bark there, and Sid gets it.' Then he suggested, 'He forgets to leave the bark.' This was the point at which he had 'pumped myself dry'[13] and found that 'at page 400 of my manuscript the story made a sudden and determined halt and refused to proceed another step.'[14]

If the note was merely to contain the message, 'We ain't dead – we are only off playing pirates,' the author's ruminations over what would happen to it were completely out of proportion. If Tom left Jackson's Island to deliver this message and then return, the bequest of his proudest possessions to Joe Harper was equally absurd. If, as one of the notes suggested, he was to forget to leave the scroll after swimming part of the river and sneaking under his aunt's bed, he would be completely unbelievable. But if the bark was to contain a farewell message to Aunt Polly and was to be stolen by Sid, this scene might prepare for Tom's return at age thirty seven to St Petersburg. Though the possible development of the plot is conjectural, it is plausible to suggest an identification scene, perhaps a court trial, in which the stolen bark would be the crucial evidence. . . .[15]

Used in one way, the plot would continue on the course Twain outlined on the first page of his manuscript; used in another, the direction of the novel would be altered.

Twain chose not to have Tom start his travels. The boy returns the scroll to his jacket pocket, where Aunt Polly discovers it a few chapters later. It was undoubtedly after he made the decision that he also turned back to page 401 and inserted a paragraph: 'This was Wednesday night. If the other (then on the back page) continued missing until Sunday, all hope would be given over & the funeral would be preached on that morning. Tom shuddered.' *Now,* the stage was set for the boys' return to their own funeral.

In several places the author reminded himself marginally to insert Aunt Polly's discovery of the message: on page 409 he jotted down 'The piece of bark at Aunt Polly's,' and on page 464, 'Aunt P's bark.' Finally, on manuscript page 512 he related her discovery of the scroll and rounded off the awkward solution of that problem. He never explained Tom's similar message to Joe or his strange bequest of his 'treasures' to his friend. Whether from expediency, indifference, or, most likely, the realisation that Tom Sawyer was not the boy to send off on the 'Battle of Life in many lands,' Twain decided not to start Tom's journeying. Evidence that he realised Tom's shortcomings for such a role is offered by his own statement to Howells that 'by and by I shall take a boy of twelve and run him on through life (in the first person) but not Tom Sawyer – he would not be a good character for it.'[16] The decision committed him to centre the book in his protagonist's boyhood in St Petersburg. □

This decision not to have Tom grow up has a significance reaching beyond *Tom Sawyer* itself. In his own novel Huck Finn does not grow up, and we may want to question Twain's ability to deal directly with the experience of mature adults. Related to this issue is the recurrent concentration in American literature on youth or adolescence. Rejecting the life-patterns of European culture (heterosexual marriage, the family), it seems American literature is not confident about what other structures there might be. Other than becoming rich (the end of *Tom Sawyer*) what is there to grow up into?

Hill continues by detailing other re-arrangements of the second half of the book:

■ . . . it appears that Twain originally intended the picnic section to follow the scene in which Tom took Becky's whipping.[17] Then Muff Potter's trial was substituted. While writing of the after effects of Muff's trial, Twain cancelled a passage which was to lead to the capture or death of Injun Joe. In chapter XXIV, just before the final sentence of the published book, he wrote regarding Tom's apprehension of Injun Joe's revenge: 'But Providence lifts even a boy's burden when it begins to get too heavy for him. The angel sent to attend to Tom's was an old back-country farmer named Ezra Ward, who had been a schoolmate of Aunt Polly's so many . . .' The page (MS p.600) ended and Twain discarded whatever other pages carried the idea further. Ezra Ward became an enigma, the only clue to his intended function in the story being the cryptic marginal note, 'Brick pile.' At this spot, probably, Twain replaced whatever plan he had for Injun Joe with the 'buried treasure' chapters culminating in Joe's death in the cave. For he began writing the treasure chapters (XXV–XXIX) immediately after cancelling the 'Ezra Ward' material. These chapters then followed the trial chapter, and the beginning of the picnic was placed in chapter XXIX. At this point, apparently realising the climactic possibilities of the cave chapters, Twain placed the two sections on the graduation exercises and on the Cadets of Temperance between the whipping scene and Potter's trial. This manipulation of material which was written more or less at random was accurately described by Brander Matthews:

> When at last he became convinced that he had made his profit out of every possible reminiscence, he went over what he had written with great care, adjusting the several instalments one to the other, sometimes transposing a chapter or two and sometimes writing into the earlier chapters the necessary preparation for adventures in the later chapters unforeseen when he was engaged on the beginnings of the book.[18]

Furthermore, this rearrangement of his material tends to support the theory that Twain was working with the deliberate intention of showing Tom's maturation. The school graduation depicting the high jinks at the expense of the school master and the painfully amateurish orations, and the Cadets of Temperance material revealing a youthful, irresolute Tom Sawyer were inserted in a relatively early spot in the manuscript, forcing three of the four chapters which Blair suggests are crucial into later positions.[19] The trial of Muff Potter was followed by the treasure chapters which portrayed a superstitious and fanciful pair of boys, and before this line of action was completed in chapter XXIV by 'showing Huck conquering fear to rescue the widow',[20] the author inserted some preliminary paragraphs originating the picnic scene, paragraphs which had originally been intended for chapter XXI. Next came Huck's bravery (MS pp.706–21), completing the Injun Joe line of action. Finally the picnic material developed into the adventures in the cave, which not only completed the Tom and Becky line of action but also showed Tom at his most manly. Though terms like *maturation, boyhood, youth,* and *early manhood* are ambiguous and ill-defined, nevertheless the rearranging of these climactic chapters allowed Twain to present Tom in a group of critical situations toward the end of the book where maturer judgement and courage were vital. These events required a Tom Sawyer who was nowhere apparent in the idyllic first half of the book. □

It is true that Tom is more mature in the scenes Hill points to than in other incidents. This occurrence, however, may have more to do with the 'Tom' these scenes necessitate than with any realistic process of development in the character. Like Huck Finn in the later novel, Tom changes according to the occasion because he is as much a means of access to the range of his author's experience as he is a consistent character. *Tom Sawyer* leaves us with a pre-pubescent Tom and Becky, and what are at best a series of propositions for Tom's future. Maturity in this context is notional.

Nearly twenty years before Hill, Bernard DeVoto had frankly accepted that, whatever Twain's intentions, it was futile to attempt to schematise *Tom Sawyer*. His *Tom Sawyer* is also more unsettled than Howells' and it has limitations which DeVoto, though he acclaims Twain, immediately acknowledges. The gravest of them,

■ is that the boys are of no particular age and therefore much that they do and feel is psychological anachronism. Howells's partly indecipherable comment on chapter III, 'Tom is either too old for that or too young for . . .' is true of the books as a whole. Precisely as the story takes place in a year that has no anchorage in time (well, if pedants must, it is not later than 1845 – and therefore, since Mark was born in 1835, Tom has not yet reached his tenth birthday), so the emotions of boyhood swing through half a dozen ages. The sham battle, the forest outlawry, the mischief of the school scenes, the treasure-digging and the cure of warts are proper to the age of eight or nine. But Tom's adoration of Becky is nearer adolescence, and the boys who camp on Jackson's Island, shadow Injun Joe, want to take a drink when forbidden by the pledge, minister to Muff Potter in jail, and save the Widow Douglas are twelve or thirteen. Surely Tom can be no younger than that, may even be older, when he testifies in court and comforts Becky in the cave.

Finally, though the book is more profoundly true to the phantasies of boyhood than any other ever written, and to maturity's nostalgia for what it once was, though it has forged the symbols that seem likely to express boyhood more permanently than any other in literature, it cannot be thought of as comprehensive or profound realism. The term is dangerous; certainly the forged symbol transcends literalism and the truth of *Tom Sawyer* is the kind of truth that only symbols can express – like the symbols of *Antigone* or those of *Macbeth*. But you need only differentiate boyhood from its symbols to perceive how much of it Mark ignores. There is, we have seen, no sex – none of the curiosity, the shame, the torment, the compulsion of young ignorance groping in mystery. Becky and Tom in the empty schoolroom do not belong in the same world with any pair of ten-year-olds in a hayloft, and though Tom thinking of her by the dark river is profoundly true he never goes on to think of her as any boy must in the years when girls are last known to be females. 'Such things were not even dreamed of in that society.'

Furthermore, Tom's immortal daydreams never get much above the childish level. Piracy, highway robbers, the outlaws of the forest, the circus, the vagabondage of Jackson's Island – yes, thank God. But was there no glance forward as well, had he no nebulous, inarticulate vision of growing up, did he get no nearer than this to the threshold of ambition and desire, where boyhood darkly flowers in frustrated poetry? Has a boy no griefs and losses outside of phantasy, no satisfactions and no achievements more real than these? Is a boy's mind no wider and no deeper than Tom's? Where are the brutalities, the sternnesses, the strengths, the perceptions, and the failures that will eventually make a man; Well, in part Mark's will was to ignore such things, as when he denies us the entire struggle of fear, pity, and horror out of which Tom's decision to reveal what he had seen in the graveyard issues, in order to give us the simple melodrama of the revelation. And in part he was incapable of the analysis which the probing of motives and psychological intricacies requires: his understanding was intuitive and concrete and he was sure only of behaviour, fumbling when he had to be introspective.

So with St Petersburg, the society in which Tom's summer is played out. What is asserted of it is all memorably trite but much has been left out. Mark was to go on and tell the rest in other books, but there the society was formed out of nostalgia and the book became a pastoral poem, an idyll of an America that had already vanished when it was written. And by now it must be clear that, though there is also a direct answer to the doubts we have expressed, this discussion has so far been conducted on false premises.[21] □

Whether or not half a dozen is the number, DeVoto is right to point to Tom's various ages and thus develop the point hinted at by the last reviewer above. Nor does he want to make Howells' kind of claim for *Tom Sawyer*'s realism. 'There is . . . no sex' in the Becky–Tom relationship, an ingredient which for DeVoto (and for us?) would inevitably be there in real life. How much Twain, even indirectly or by implication, can deal with sexuality remains an insistent question. It relates to DeVoto's point about Tom's lack of a vision of 'growing up' and more generally to the point already made above about Twain's ability to present mature experience. DeVoto's term 'nostalgia' bears also on these matters, in so far as it may be a longing for a more innocent untroubled time. How central a motive was nostalgia to Twain's recurrent recreations of that village on the banks of the Mississippi, the Hannibal, Missouri of his boyhood?

But DeVoto spent a lifetime celebrating Twain and his important reservations about the writer, especially in the last sentence in the second paragraph above, are the springboard for acclamation:

■ For the discussion leaves out what millions of readers have experienced in the sixty-six years since *Tom Sawyer* was published. No book can become world literature, as this one has become, unless it has authority over the imagination of mankind, and such authority makes merely idle the kind of doubt expressed here. It is a complex thing but the basis of it is that it embodies universal phantasies. When Tom triumphs in the whitewashing, enacts the death of Robin Hood, is punished for his beloved's fault, establishes his pirates' den on Jackson Island, and dramatically insures justice to Muff Potter, the dreams of all childhood everywhere are fulfilled in him. 'I wish I had been on that island,' Howells said and the same wish, known or only felt, has been wakened and gratified in everyone who ever read the book. It is a deep wish for natural beauty and daring adventure, for dawn and midnight storm and flowing river, and underneath that for all the freedoms that the soul needs. It is at the very core of desire. But darker needs are also voiced and allayed. The book's enchantment is so strong that it beguiles one into forgetting how much of the spell issues from dread and horror. The story pivots on body-snatching, revenge, murder, robbery, drowning, starvation, and the fear of death. It exists in a medium darkened by witchcraft and demonology, ghosts are only an amulet's width away; the malevolence of the unseen world is everywhere a danger as tangible as Injun Joe. All these give it primary drama – but also they crystallise, more perfectly than any-where else in literature, the terrors that are as indissolubly a part of boyhood as the reflex of freedom. If Mark could not analyse the ferments of the mind's dark side, he has given them enduring symbols. Tom writhing with guilt during a thunderstorm; Tom and Huck cowering behind the trees while murder is done and then, in darkness and moonlight, hearing Bull Harbison howl above Muff Potter who will surely die; Tom and Huck preserved from death only by the collapse of a stairway that Injun Joe is mounting; Tom and Becky wandering in the cave with dwindling candle and then await-ing death in darkness; the half-breed chipping at the sill in the knowledge that he must die – these and many other images are an ecstasy from the soul's fear, and boyhood finds in them a richer, deeper expression than literature has elsewhere given it. The symbols speak for millions out of the shadow of unbodied dread.

In this way *Tom Sawyer* transcends realism, transcends its narrative, transcends its characters and becomes mythology. No actual boy ever filled his pockets with fees paid for the privilege of whitewashing a fence, or followed the pathway of terror from an opened grave to treasure buried under a cross. The way of fact is the curve of an arc; myth, like poetry, travels straight across, on the chord. Millions have assented as Tom Sawyer moves along the chord, and millions more will assent. He is a universal myth, a part of the small store of truth that American literature has added to the treasure of mankind. . . .

As such it perfectly preserves something of the American experience, more of American dreaming, and still more of the beauty that was our heritage and that still conditions both our national memory and our phantasy. On one side of it is Cardiff Hill, a remnant of the great forest, on the other side is the great river: both at the very base of our awareness. Between these beauties the village is sleepy, peaceful, and secure. The world invades it only as romance and adventure; the energies of the age are over the horizon. Time has stopped short; the frontier has passed by and the industrial revolution is not yet born. Life is confident and untroubled, moves serenely at an unhurried pace, fulfills itself in peace. Islanded in security, in natural beauty, St Petersburg is an idyll of what we once were, of what it is now more than ever necessary to remember we once were. Here also the book captures and will keep secure forever a part of America – of America over the hills and far away. □

'It embodies universal fantasies'; 'the dreams of all childhood everywhere are fulfilled'; 'the terrors that are as indisputably a part of boyhood as the reflex of freedom'. These are large claims which readers must test for themselves. One test, suggested by the term boyhood, is to ask how gender specific, in a limiting sense, Twain's engagement with experience in *Tom Sawyer* is. More generally, is Twain likely to appeal to men rather than women, because he has a rather undeveloped sense of women's possibilities? DeVoto's pointing to the 'dread and horror' in *Tom Sawyer* alerts us to ingredients only the third reviewer above has so far hinted at. They mix uneasily with any nostalgic drive in Twain and make us aware how all his energies are subject to thrust and counterthrust. Returning to the question of realism, DeVoto asserts *Tom Sawyer* transcends this mode and 'becomes mythology'. Again a large claim which may become vapid by the time DeVoto, as an American, is claiming 'St Petersburg is an idyll of what we once were, of what it is now more than ever necessary to remember we once were'. DeVoto's book is published during the Second World War. How remembrance of *Tom Sawyer* would succour during conflict on that scale is not made clear. There is, as we shall see, powerful racial conflict in the novel, together with the communal need to demonise a human being who is different from the majority.

Dwight MacDonald is impatient with the kind of past America chooses to indulge:

■ . . . Our national past is now very much in fashion. Not the past of our classical period, the early republic of Jefferson and Madison and Adams, and not the Gilded Age – to use a term coined by Mark Twain – of Grant and Rockefeller and McKinley. Either of these might be instructive, the first as a tradition, the second as a warning. But what is wanted is romance rather than instruction, a past to escape into, not a past to learn from. So the vogue is for the forty-niners, the Civil War, the frontier, the Wild West. The editors of *Life* have celebrated the Winning of the West in seven instalments, some of the most popular television shows are Westerns, and a six-shooter is now as prosaic a utensil as an egg beater; all publishing is divided into three parts – fiction, non-fiction, and Civil War; Carl Sandburg, the good gray laureate of the hinterland, has intoned a Lincoln's Birthday address, full of piety and glucose, to a hushed session of Congress . . . since we no longer feel very young or optimistic or great-hearted, we yearn for the myth of the frontier.[22] ☐

Tom Sawyer in MacDonald's view contributes to this need for romance. It is Twain's 'best-loved book – for poor reasons'. Tom is

■ the All-American Boy. He tries to avoid washing, he resists medicine, he plays hooky, he teases the cat, he patronises the old (ole) swimming (swimmin') hole, he squirms in church, he wriggles in school, he is ritualistically absurd in love, he is fertile in mischief. By page 2, Aunt Polly is saying, 'I never did see the beat of that boy!' By page 3, 'He's full of the Old Scratch!' The first chapters are fascinating, for here, as in the first glimpses of Sherlock Holmes in *A Study in Scarlet,* we can see a mass-culture hero taking form. The sureness with which Twain builds up the cliché is something to be admired (or deplored). One of Tom's most endearing (or irritating) qualities is his love of romantic mystification. He is a general, a Robin Hood, a pirate: 'There comes a time in every rightly constructed boy's life when he has a raging desire to go somewhere and dig for hidden treasure. This desire came upon Tom one day. He sallied out. . . .' Tom can't even lose a tooth without adding to the cliché: 'But all trials bring their compensations. As Tom wended to school after breakfast, he was the envy of every boy he met because the gap in his upper row of teeth enabled him to expectorate in a new and admirable way.' There is a lot of 'fine' writing in *Tom Sawyer*. Sometimes, as in 'sallied out,' 'wended,' and 'expectorate,' it is ironic; describing boyhood trivia in inflated language is, or was, a reliable comic device. More often, it is the kind of stylistic lapse one often finds in Whitman, another self-taught folk writer. The folk tradition had become feeble by the second half of the nineteenth century, and naive geniuses were more open to corruption by the elegant rhetoric of their time than they would have been a century earlier. So one gets sentences like 'The two boys flew on and on, toward the village, speechless with horror. . . . The barkings of the aroused watchdogs seemed to give wings to their feet.' ☐

A 'mass-culture hero' whose 'rebellion is phoney', *Tom Sawyer* for MacDonald is America's comfort blanket, its author settling for fine language as much as he mocks it. Developing the contrasts with *Huckleberry Finn*, MacDonald reflects on information other critics are also to ponder:

■ it is interesting that Twain originally tried to write *Tom Sawyer,* too, in the first person. In *Mark Twain at Work*, DeVoto prints a very early draft, twenty pages long, which he found among the Mark Twain papers. It is first-person and it makes dreary reading, 'cute' and contrived; Twain just didn't feel at home inside a middle-class boy. He was quite right to do *Tom Sawyer* in the third person. For Tom is too respectable, too close to what Twain had become after his literary success and his marriage to the daughter of the leading coal dealer of Elmira, New York. □

But surely it was Clemens, not the invented Twain, who married into respectability. Moreover, tensions between Clemens and Twain, complicated further by tensions between Twain and a Huck, or Twain and a Hank Morgan, energised the fiction. As for doing *Tom Sawyer* in a third person Mark Twain voice, this was surely Clemens' attempt to objectify his own experience. Indulged as it is, this experience was all too likely to collapse into subjectivity and sentimentality had it been delivered by Tom in the first person, since Tom himself is clearly a version of the young Clemens. In the later novel, by contrast, Huck Finn's voice is as far from Clemens as Clemens was ever able to get. With it there is little risk of mere authorial subjectivity.

Alfred Kazin begins his response to *Tom Sawyer* from a similar position to MacDonald's. He is exploring the relationship between Twain's created present and re-created past:

■ Mark Twain said that the book was 'simply a hymn, put into prose to give it a worldly air.' But when Howells, who counselled that the book be directed to children, allowed himself to wonder 'why we hate the past so,' his friend responded from the depths, 'It's so humiliating.'

The forty-year-old who composed *Tom Sawyer* in 1875–76 was far from his boyhood poverty and the old Southwest but not from the vehement uncertainties that were as much a mark of his character as his aggressive humour. The author of that 'hymn' had become perhaps the most commercially successful author in America; his books were sold by a network of subscription agents who were hard to turn away from the door. He was one of the most public characters in America; somehow everyone knew how happy and prosperous Mark Twain was as he doted on his wife and four children and 'humorously' complained of what it cost him to keep up in Hartford the large, overdecorated, ornately stuffed Victorian mansion. The house was another one of Mark Twain's many fantasies come to life. It had everything that the genteel tradition required of a successful man, but like Mark Twain himself for all his heartburnings, it was also defiantly up-to-date. It was the first house in Hartford with a telephone; Mark Twain was the first eminent American writer to possess a typewriter. There was a large staff; their flamboyant employer alternately boasted and cringed at what his servants cost him when he compared his laundry woman's wages with what his family in Hannibal had lived on. The Hartford enclave, Nook Farm, was literary, prosperous, clerical – 'the quality' to the life. For a poor and once 'shiftless' boy who at thirteen had been apprenticed to the local newspapers, and at eighteen had started his wandering career as a printer in St Louis, New York, Philadelphia, Muscatine, Keokuk, and Cincinnati, Mark Twain at forty was certainly that post-Civil War type, 'the man who has risen.'

And he had done it all through words – which at times made him feel that everything he had gained by quicksilver cleverness, the stage drawl and the platform manner, was unreal. His life resembled a work of fiction made by works of fiction. He already had a disposition to think of his life as a 'dream' – the American dream, of course, but one that also revealed a writer's tendency to wonder whether the thoughts and projects that occupied him day and night had any existence outside himself. At the end of his 'wonderful century' whose many wonders he personified to his countrymen, he was to write in *The Mysterious Stranger* that the universe itself was a dream, thus rounding out a century of American solipsism.

In Nook Farm, Hannibal itself became a dream. The proud, opulent, but endlessly reminiscent Mark Twain was writing *Tom Sawyer* in the smug atmosphere of post-war Republicanism; the ragged Confederate volunteer was now a favourite orator at reunions of the Grand Army of the Republic. He could not help touching up the past, to the point where it would all come back less humiliating. But he now invented the past more than he renovated it. After all, *Tom Sawyer* was his first real novel.

Post-war America was already looking to the 'old West' for a golden age. Our now-celebrated author had revisited Hannibal on a sentimental journey; he had gone up and down the great river to write his utterly sunshot pieces for the *Atlantic Monthly* on learning to be a steamboat pilot, 'Old Times on the Mississippi.' The undestroyed vividness of his old associations amazed him. Had he ever left Hannibal?

The things about me and before me made me feel like a boy again – convinced me that I was a boy again, and that I had been simply

> dreaming an unusually long dream. . . . During my three days' stay in the town, I woke up every morning with the impression that I was a boy – for in my dreams the faces were all young again, and looked as they had looked in the old times.
>
> He recognised the melancholy limitations of his old life – how remote and isolated a village like 'St Petersburg' in *Tom Sawyer* could be. . . .[23] □

The past that Twain found 'so humiliating' emerges in *The Innocents Abroad* where the failure of humanity to achieve lasting happiness, peace, justice, and any certainty is a recurrent note. In the Holy Land, Christianity's most revered locations are themselves arenas of religious strife. Vesuvius's gratuitous obliteration of Pompeii confirms the futility of the human lot. There is a sense that past, in all its magnitude, pre-empts the New World future, revealing the delusion of New World optimism.

Only through his humour can Twain find relief. His humour can mock and deride and insult the past, freeing the New World from its burden. The humour affirms the belief, always so necessary to national self-confidence, that there *is* an exemplary New World.

The self-created Mark Twain, as Kazin sees it, embodies this world with all its latest gadgets. In *Tom Sawyer* it is provided with a past which is not humiliating, a past blending easily with 'the smug atmosphere of post-war Republicanism' in which Twain himself was a triumphant figure. Kazin continues:

■ With *Tom Sawyer* – the first of his books to show him entirely as objective storyteller – he capitalised on his early life. Before *Huckleberry Finn*, he had no greater story to tell than one about an irrepressibly imaginative boy who could make other boys submit to his (book-learned) fantasies.

It was a story to be told at a comfortable remove. The archness fitted the benevolence of middle-aged successes toward their younger selves, of urban leaders toward the old farm and the rustic village. Heavily Victorian Americans could feel that America was still young. Now that the dire Calvinist suspicions that children were as damnable as everyone else were done away with, boys and girls emerged sweet and cute, loveable and cherishable – as nice and as good, in short, as grown-up Americans.

The growing comfort and self-satisfaction of middle-class life made happy families dote on their children as never before. There was little religious consolation when they died – Mark Twain was to lose three, and the death of one particularly beloved daughter at twenty-four was a shock he never got over. Anxiety in prosperity made the now-loveable American child as significant a type as the 'shrewd' self-respecting Yankee. The child in popular American literature becomes a dear little fellow, the loveable urchin and 'scamp,' the professional 'bad boy.' These were milksops turned inside out, future leaders of American enterprise, from Thomas Bailey Aldrich's Tom Bailey to Booth Tarkington's Penrod.

One began to miss the clairvoyant Pearl in *The Scarlet Letter*. That child of sin had a cool and deadly Puritan eye for concealment. What simpleminded 'rascals' barefoot American boys become in the illustrations to children's books, as they skip off to the ole fishing hole in a frayed straw hat and with one gallus trailing down their torn pants. What little darlings girls become in their yellow curls and starched ruffles – what 'spirit' they show in the face of adversity! Perhaps nowhere as in New England, with its race pride making up for its loss of moral authority, were so many children's books manufactured for magazines like *Youth's Companion, St Nicholas, Riverside Magazine for Young People, Wide Awake, Our Young Folks.* No wonder that Mark Twain, at ease in Hartford, got into the game. Nowhere else did comfortableness with one's racial, social, religious, and financial well-being get itself complacently expressed in so many images of the *manly, sturdy, bright,* and *cheery* Protestant boy. Thomas Bailey Aldrich in *The Story of a Bad Boy:* 'an amiable, impulsive lad, blessed with fine digestive powers, and no hypocrite . . . in short, I was a real human boy, such as you may meet anywhere in New England, and no more like the impossible boy in a storybook than a sound orange is like one that has been sucked dry.'

No wonder that Mark Twain in Connecticut remembered the raw Missouri of the 1850s so fondly in *Tom Sawyer* as a place where children had no life but play. Of course he could not decide until the last moment whether this idyll, this hymn put into prose to give it a worldly air, was for children or adults. Howells, who knew the middle road in all things (until in the darkening nineties he grew weary of the Establishment and moved to New York), persuaded his friend to call *Tom Sawyer* a children's book. And it was Howells who had him remove innocent bits of real life from the novel (Becky sneaking a look at a naked body in teacher's anatomy text) as 'awful good but too dirty.' Howells always knew what the public would take, and he wrote straight *to* this public, whose inquiring photographer in fiction he was for so long that he felt he had been created by the reading public. □

Here we are reminded of *Tom Sawyer*'s place in studies of the literature of childhood and of the shaping of children to confirm adult self-image.

Preconceptions about gender rear their heads, as in Howells' decision about Becky.

Kazin indicates how close Tom must have been to the young Sam Clemens:

■ Mark Twain as a famous author confessed that he did not care to read fiction. The young Sam Clemens in Hannibal must have read himself sick on stories of pirates, Robin Hood, medieval knights and ladies. (He was always romantic about the Middle Ages.) Tom Sawyer represents the future author's greatest fantasy: to turn life into a book. Of course there is a good deal of routine, boys-will-be-boys mischief. 'And when she closed with a happy Scriptural flourish, he "hooked" a doughnut.' Tom must get the best of every encounter, confrontation, negotiation. Sceptics may see a future corporation type in Tom's ability to swap his inferior store of boy's goods – 'twelve marbles, part of a Jew's harp, a piece of blue bottle-glass to look through . . . a dog-collar but no dog' – for stuff slightly less inferior. His chief trait, which leads to his many (sometimes unbearable) intrigues, is his unquestioned sense of himself as guide and leader to every other boy in town. He is a born dominator, for he is totally – as young Sam Clemens must have been – at the mercy of his imagination. Whatever he has read of that world beyond the village, in which pirates and Robin Hood and medieval knights act out some 'gorgeous' code, Tom himself must act out. Other boys follow him because they can no more resist Tom's wild fancy than we can resist Mark Twain's.

The most famous episode in *Tom Sawyer* – Tom's persuading his friends to pay him for the 'privilege' of whitewashing Aunt Polly's fence – can be believed only if you recognise what a power of fantasy drives this mighty spieler. Tom can talk people into anything because no one else really shares, much less understands, his determination to live by the book. This gives him a power over them that reminds us of an author's power.

From his guardian, Aunt Polly, on down, the adults in St Petersburg must also participate in the book Tom is acting out; they are the chorus, plaintive but unavailing, as Tom goes through his adventures. □

One of Tom's functions for Twain is to be a portrait of the artist as a young boy. In this connection it is noteworthy that he is associated primarily with fantasy and escapism, especially as Twain himself liked to test other people's art according to simple realistic theories; see for example his denunciations of great Italian painters in *The Innocents Abroad* and his hilarious essay 'Fenimore Cooper: Literary Offenses'. His own commitment to the realistic is evident in the reportage and documentation in

Roughing It and in much of the dialogue and several of the incidents in *Huckleberry Finn*. Even so, fantasy plays a part in all of his books and is the motivating energy of several of them, for example *The Prince and the Pauper* (1882) and *A Connecticut Yankee* (1889). His continuing implication in Tom Sawyer's kind of imagination is demonstrated by the fact that adventures associated with Tom fascinated him, after *Huckleberry Finn*, in *Tom Sawyer Abroad* (1894) and *Tom Sawyer Detective* (1896). Always the romanticist and realist in him were in tension. Ultimately this tension belonged to the divide between imagination and reality which had its own force in nineteenth century American literature, since its writers were unsustained by established traditions bridging the divide.

As have other critics, Kazin emphasises Howells' restraining of *Tom Sawyer* and hints that Twain's wife Olivia ('Livy') may also have curbed his more radical energies. Walter Blair presents a more balanced picture, at least as far as *Tom Sawyer* is concerned:

■ Two manuscripts of *Tom Sawyer* have survived, and have been studied. The original at Georgetown University, Washington, D.C., shows no signs of Livy's censorship, though it does indicate that she took the trouble to remind her husband to have Tom take Becky's spanking for her in chapter XX and to have the cat snatch off the master's wig in chapter XXI. If she suggested bowdlerisations, the manuscript does not show where.[24]

The amanuensis copy now in Jefferson City, Missouri, was made after Livy had offered whatever suggestions she had. But this manuscript contains passages later deleted. Also it shows Howells at work. Clemens had met Howells in 1869, after the latter had favourably reviewed *Innocents Abroad* for the *Atlantic* . . .

In 1872, when Howells appreciatively reviewed *Roughing It*, Clemens wrote: 'I'm as uplifted and reassured by it as a mother who had given birth to a white baby when she was awfully afraid that it was going to be a mulatto.'[25] Howells also won Clemens' gratitude by urging him to write for the *Atlantic*. As their friendship grew, Clemens depended increasingly on Howells' literary judgements. Clemens talked with his friend about *Tom Sawyer* in the summer of 1875 and possibly accepted suggestions. Later, when Howells read the completed manuscript, he suggested it be published 'explicitly as a boy's book,' and Clemens, as the preface shows, agreed. It must be strongly emphasised that Howells had a juvenile audience in mind, therefore, when he 'made some corrections and suggestions in a faltering pencil – almost all in the first third,'[26] and that it was with such an audience in mind that the author accepted them.

Most, indisputably, were stylistic.[27] But the humorist 'tamed all the obscenities until I judged that they no longer carried offense.'

Only three passages were involved. The poodle which sat on the pinchbug in church (chapter V) originally 'went sailing up the aisle with his tail shut down like a hasp.' Howells, having spotted an indecency which I have been able to find with the kind help of a colleague, wrote, 'Awfully good but a little too dirty,' and the last eight words were deleted. A more extensive change was made in chapter XX, where Becky stole a peek at the schoolmaster's book and found a picture of 'a human figure, stark naked.' Howells commented, 'I should be afraid of this picture incident.' Twain excised Tom's explanation, 'How could *I* know it wasn't a nice book? I didn't know girls ever –' He deleted Becky's plaint that she would suffer worse punishments than whipping: 'But that isn't anything – it ain't *half*. You'll tell everybody about this picture, and O,O,O!' Becky's thought, 'He'll tell the scholars about that hateful picture – maybe he's told some of them before now,' was removed. So was part of Tom's soliloquy on 'what a curious kind of a fool a girl is': 'But that picture – is – well, now it ain't so curious she feels bad about that. . . . No, I reckon it ain't. Suppose she was Mary and Alf Temple had caught her looking at such a picture as that and went around telling. She'd feel – well, I'd lick him. I bet I would. . . . Then Dobbins would tell his wife about the picture.' The third refinement made at Howells' suggestion was the deletion of one of Huck's less elegant complaints about Widow Douglas' civilising him (chapter XXXV): 'she'd gag when I spit.' These were the moral improvements which Howells urged, and weep for them though we may, they do not seem disastrous or very frustrating. They made sense in a book for juveniles in a society which would ban the book from some libraries even after these concessions.[28] □

The untroubled racism Twain could share with Howells in responding to the review of *Roughing It* is at least as noteworthy as everything else in the above piece. On the issue of Twain's submission to censorship, Blair concludes:

■ But there is much reason to doubt that at this time the writer was constantly – even frequently – enraged because he was checked. A noteworthy fact is that he himself initiated the most famous change in *Tom Sawyer*, after Livy, her aunt, her mother, and Howells had approved the passage involved. Should Huck, he asked in a letter, 'in a book now professedly and confessedly a boy's and girl's book,' use a phrase that never bothered the author 'until I had ceased to regard the volume as being for adults' – should he complain that the widow's servants 'comb me all to hell?' Howells answered that he supposed he had missed the phrase 'because the locution was so familiar to my Western sense, and so exactly what Huck would say.' 'But,' he added, 'it won't do for children.' Huck was duly combed 'all to thunder.' Nor was this the only passage Twain himself thought needed softening. 'Satan' became 'the devil'; 'foul slop,' 'water'; 'reeking,' 'drenched.' And in chapter XXIX he changed Injun Joe's recipe for revenge on a woman, 'you cut her nose off – and her ears,' to the more genteel (though still somewhat unmannerly) 'You slit her nostrils – you notch her ears like a sow!'

These revisions on the author's own initiative provide the strong possibility that if Livy or Howells had not suggested some changes, he may well have made them on his own. For he not only eagerly sought instruction in matters of taste: whatever the reason, he himself was carefully conventional about many matters, and in writing for publication (though not in private conversations or correspondence) he prudishly limited his treatment of sex. This meant that some important aspects of life would not be treated well or at length in his published works. □

Prudish tendencies Twain undoubtedly had, yet Blair himself is evasive in his response to Injun Joe's revenge intentions towards a woman. 'Somewhat unmannerly' hardly describes Injun Joe's appalling proposal.

Perhaps Kazin had this proposal in mind, when he concluded his essay by finding evil in *Tom Sawyer* embodied in 'the villainous half-breed Injun Joe'. It is 'the background necessary to comedy' and 'is defeated. Wickedness in the person of Injun Joe dies of starvation in the cave.' Inexorably we are moving towards a study of this outcast's contribution to the novel. Decades before Kazin, James M. Cox had already shown that it was not as simple as Kazin propounds. Cox begins by offering another version of the structure of the novel:

■ The most striking aspect of *Tom Sawyer* is its almost total lack of plot in the conventional sense of that word. There is little or no transition between episodes; continuity results from appearance and reappearance of the same characters. The most obvious defence of this lack of causal sequence – plot as machinery – is that it reinforces the pervasive determinism of Tom Sawyer's world. Although Tom reacts to the daily occurrences which confront him and although he makes belated attempts to meet his fate, he is quite powerless to initiate the action.

The real unity of *Tom Sawyer* arises not so much from the underlying determinism as from the insistent rhythm of the novel, a rhythm based upon repetition and variation of central motives. The violence and terror which are just beneath the surface of the boys' world regularly erupt into it. After the pleasures of the schoolroom comes the dark and unknown night, bringing with it fear and death.[29] □

Pleasure and fear, life and death; repetition and variation of these themes are the keys to Cox's reading of the novel:

■ Adding to this rhythmic structure and reinforcing the unity is, of course, the central character of Tom. Walter Blair, a Mark Twain specialist who attempted a conventional explanation of the structure of *Tom Sawyer* contended that the novel deals with a boy's growth, but instead of analysing the psychology of that growth he wandered away from his fertile suggestion and divided the novel into rather useless structural units. The novel is indeed about growing up. Appearing first merely as a Bad Boy, Tom, as Mr Blair points out, develops into a character of real interest. His humour has been much discussed, its sources have been thoroughly examined, but the psychology behind it has often been neglected. Tom's repeated death fantasies are nowhere scrutinised by the scholars who have so painstakingly provided a 'background' for the novel, yet these very fantasies give Tom's character depth and complexity. Time after time the rhythm of the novel is expressed in terms of his death wish. Tom retires into solitude envisioning the mourning of the village when its inhabitants realise that he is no more. The culmination of the Jackson Island episode is the triumphal return of Tom and his two cronies to witness their own funerals. Even when death closes in on Tom and Becky in the darkness of the cave, Tom awaits it with a certain pleasure.

But there is another death, a death brutal and ghastly, lurking just beyond the boys' world and constantly impinging on it; it is the death in the graveyard and the death of Injun Joe – instead of warmth and protection this death is informed with terror. To see it as a brutal fact waiting in the adult world is to look with wistful eyes at that other death. The cave episode, fantastic from a 'realistic' point of view, is oddly appropriate because it embodies the paradox of death and isolation; it is in the cave that Tom, in the very arms of the warm shadow, manages to find the will to force his way to light and safety, but it is also in the cave that Injun Joe meets one of the most violent and horrifying deaths in our literature. The two images of death are united in the cave, and it is hardly pure coincidence that Injun Joe, the demon who has haunted Tom's dreams, lies dead at the sealed doorway of the abyss from which Tom has escaped. Tom has, albeit unconsciously, experienced what Hans Castorp more consciously experienced in the snowstorm: he has glimpsed the sheer terror at the centre of his childhood image of death. His immediate return to the cave to seize the treasure suggests his inner triumph.

The discovery of the treasure, significantly hidden under Injun Joe's cross, enables Tom to enter heroically the ranks of the respectable. Of course, he has been slyly respectable all along. Even when he breaks the law he does so with the intimate knowledge that he is expected to break it. His acute dramatic sense enables him to see the part he is to play, and he is therefore constantly aware of his participation in sacred social rites. This awareness results in a kind of compulsive badness in his nature: he achieves the Frommian ideal of wanting to do what society expects him to do. As the curtain drops there is triumphant confirmation of Tom's membership in the cult of the respectable. He is even trying to sell the club to Huck, cautioning him to remain a member of society because if one is to belong to Tom Sawyer's Outlaw Gang one must, paradoxically, obey the law. □

It is Cox who identifies the relationship between Tom's comfortable, respectable sentimentality about life and death, and Injun Joe's final meeting with the horror and terror of it all. For the one to survive, the other has to be buried deep in the unconscious, with the hope that it will rarely if ever emerge.

Tom H. Towers wants to resist all views which suggest *Tom Sawyer* is 'positive and optimistic'. He argues that the action of the novel is at odds with such readings:

■ All these views of *Tom Sawyer* suggest that it is positive and optimistic, or at least harmless, in its vision of man and the world; yet the action of the book seems at odds with that conclusion. The pranks and flirtations of the opening chapters soon give place to the midnight murder of Dr Robinson. The escape into the beatific nature of Jackson's Island ends with the destructiveness of the great storm and, on return to Aunt Polly, Tom suffers as the 'dreadful secret of the murder' becomes to him 'a chronic misery'. Nor does public confession free Tom from his visions of terror and death. Boyishly searching for treasure, he becomes involved in Injun Joe's murderous scheme against the Widow Douglas, and Becky's birthday party ends in the nightmare ordeal in the cave and the final confrontation with Joe. Despite the book's popular reputation, horror is very real in *Tom Sawyer;* and it is the horror and Tom's reaction to it that lie at the core of meaning in the novel and connect it to the dark unity of Twain's later work.

The structure of *Tom Sawyer* is defined by Tom's efforts to exchange the deadening actuality of his everyday life for a more intense, spiritually informed reality which he seeks in the graveyard, on the island, in his quest for secret treasure and with Becky in the cave. Opposed to that sought-for world is the town, which represents everything that inhibits the realisation of freedom and selfhood. The townspeople, for example, are uniformly mired in vanity and hypocrisy. In a travesty of Christian humility, the Sunday-school teachers preen themselves before Judge Thatcher. Just as he hides his baldness beneath a wig,

Dobbins, the schoolmaster, conceals a nasty prurience behind his apparent respectability – after he has bullied the children into submission, he slavers over the illustrations in his anatomy text. Not even Aunt Polly is free from vanity. Her glasses are for appearance only, and after Tom has tricked and defied her in the Jackson's Island adventure, she is angry with him only because he has allowed her to make a fool of herself before Mrs Harper.

Worse than such pretence is the systematic denial of freedom in St Petersburg, whose very name suggests authoritarian repression. Without doubt, Aunt Polly loves Tom, yet she conceives of her love chiefly as a duty to bend him to the customs of a spiritually dead society. As in the episode of the painkiller and the cat, her first rule for Tom is that he must be forbidden whatever he seems to desire. While she contemplates making Tom whitewash the fence, she muses, 'It's mighty hard to make him work Saturdays, when all the boys is having holiday, but he hates work more than he hates anything else, and I've *got* to do some of my duty by him, or I'll be the ruination of the child.' Later, when she unjustly scolds Tom after Sid has broken the sugar bowl, she suffers in her conscience, but she cannot retract her harsh words because 'she judged that this would be construed into a confession that she had been in the wrong, and discipline forbade that'.

So far as Tom and the other children are concerned, the whole of society consists in restrictive, often humiliating rules and institutions. On weekdays there is school with its floggings, and on Sundays there is the confining propriety of church. There is, of course, neither learning in the school nor salvation in the church; both institutions seem to exist only to deny spontaneous humanity. Shoes and baths are the unnatural uses of unnatural society, and there are rules against swimming and playing and talking to Huck Finn. Still worse, the life of St Petersburg is charged with cruelty and violence that result logically from the frustrations accompanying such ubiquitous repression. The first major incident in the novel is the murder of Dr Robinson by Injun Joe, and the last third of the book is concerned largely with Joe's intended assault upon the Widow Douglas. But in some ways Joe seems no more than an embodiment of the unconscious desire of St Petersburg generally. Like the landsmen in *Huck Finn* or the royal court in *Connecticut Yankee,* the towns people of this novel regard death and suffering mainly as welcome diversion. They can be stirred from their lethargy only by the prospect of lurid death – the planned lynching of Muff Potter, the supposed drowning of Tom and Huck, or the children's ordeal in the cave. Even Aunt Polly harbours a secret fascination with violence; she confesses, 'I dream about [the murder] most every night myself. Sometimes I dream it's me that done it.'[30] □

Towers is right to draw attention to the underside of village life in *Tom Sawyer*, but whether he pays sufficient attention to the entertaining terms in which Twain writes much of the novel is questionable. Also questionable are Towers' own terms, as when he speaks of Tom's search 'for a more intense, spiritually informed reality'. Does not such a pronouncement come very low on a list of things to say about Tom? Moreover is it appropriate to push *Tom Sawyer* so far towards material Twain will treat in *The Mysterious Stranger* (1916): 'the townspeople . . . are uniformly mired in vanity and hypocrisy'? Towers, however, is another critic more alive to Injun Joe than some previous critics have been. He registers that the character is not to be seen entirely as the villain: 'in some ways Injun Joe seems no more than an embodiment of the unconscious desire of St Petersburg generally'. This is a useful supplement to Cox even though it does not go as far as Cox in exploring the relationship between thesis (Tom) and antithesis (Injun Joe). Moreover, if Injun Joe embodies anyone's unconsciousness, it might well be Twain's rather than the townspeople's. Injun Joe might be the author's violent rage with all the complacency he is apparently settling for in *Tom Sawyer*.

Towers continues:

■ In nature the children intuit a spiritually vital world which seems to oppose that of adult society at every point. The town means restrictive rules and onerous tasks, but nature is the scene of games and leisure and, above all, freedom. The town is literally as well as symbolically sterile – all the women are middle-aged widows or prepubescent girls, and male sexuality is represented by Dobbins' prurience and Injun Joe's sadism. In contrast, the imagined world of the children is peopled by virile robbers and pirates, so beloved by their female captives that 'after they've been in the cave a week or two weeks they stop crying and after that . . . if you drove them out they'd turn right around and come back.' Similarly, death, which in town is at best a welcome relief from life's misery, is, in the boys' world, the prelude to new and fuller life, as when Tom and Huck seek in the graveyard symbolic renewal in the cleansing of their warts.

The disjunction between St Petersburg and the boys' world of the hills and the river is recognised in the self-conscious repudiation of the values and uses of the town when the children enter spiritualised nature. First come the ritualistic meowings and bird whistles. Then the boys must cast off their clothes, the outward signs of their social roles. (The repressive function of clothes is demonstrated in Aunt Polly's practice of sewing Tom into his shirt; conversely, it is significant that the boys must become naked not only to swim or play at Indians, but even to become robbers or circus clowns.) Finally, the boys enter into wholly new identities as they cease to be Tom or Joe and become instead Robin Hood or The Black Avenger of the Spanish Main. With their new identities comes a new impunity; thus, Tom acknowledges that his 'respectable' name, Thomas, is 'the name they lick me by' but as Robin Hood he boasts, 'I can't fall; that ain't the way it is in the book.'

The chief episodic complexes in the novel – the murder plot, the Jackson's Island scenes, the treasure hunt, and the MacDougal's Cave adventure – are unified by Tom's efforts to enter permanently this world of vitality and freedom and to escape forever the dehumanising life of St. Petersburg. To this extent *Tom Sawyer* anticipates *Huck Finn,* but there is a major and decisive difference between Tom's search for transcendence and Huck's. Each time Huck escapes from the greed and violence of society, he is reborn on the river and draws closer to the realisation of the natural morality that is eventually his salvation. With Tom the process is almost exactly inverted. Each of his withdrawals brings Tom to a fresh sense of destructive isolation and death. Huck presumably sustains his new self as he 'lights out for the territory,' but Tom ultimately renounces the equivalent of Huck's 'territory' in favour of the very community he has tried to escape throughout the book. □

Here Towers' tendency to respond to Tom's adventures in this novel as if they were Huck's in *Huckleberry Finn* is all too evident. It comes as a surprise, therefore, when he arrives where previous critics have been and sees Tom settling for 'the very community he has tried to escape'. Should not the limits of Tom's rebellion have informed Towers' reading throughout? He needs to go further also with what he says about sexuality, perceptive as this is. Why is it that Twain does sexuality in terms which hardly present a realistic account of life in a nineteenth century village on the riverbank? What investment does he have in Injun Joe's sadism towards women? Might it be a response to the roles he is convinced women demand of men, and men of women, as in the imagined behaviour in the cave? Towers takes this behaviour seriously, but primarily it is surely intended to be funny. Indeed it had better be funny, for otherwise it would be maddening. Who could stand it that relationships between male and female should be wasted in such games? And who knows what Twain's maddened imagination might like to do to those crying girls?

Injun Joe also needs to be studied in the context of the racism impinging consciously and unconsciously on all Twain's most significant writing, precisely because Twain is tainted by it. This sense of personal staining is indeed one reason his fiction avoids straightforward condemnation of racism. He is more interested in what it tells one about the self that one could be so complicit. Under conducive conditions, what might the self get implicated in? What access to transcendent moral values, assuming they exist, does the self have? Twain's racism towards Blacks up to *Tom Sawyer* and *Huckleberry Finn* is documented and explored by Arthur G. Pettit in 'Mark Twain's Attitude Toward the Negro in the West, 1861–67'[31] and in 'Mark Twain and the Negro'[32]. The first of these concludes:

■ At the close of his Western experience, however, this view of himself was still in the future: Indeed, Clemens's years in the West are important not for any change that occurred in his thinking about the Negro, but for what they tell us about the distance he had yet to travel before he reached a basically liberal view of the black man. We have seen that although Clemens decisively switched his political allegiance from the South to the North early in the Western period, his attitude toward the Negro remained essentially the same, precisely because, unlike some of his other southern traits, his Negrophobia coincided with, rather than deviated from, the Western norm. Fleeing from a terrible war, and not very interested in the survival of the Union beyond whatever impact that survival might have on his own existence, Clemens found the Far West an ideal temporary society, and a most congenial environment in which to practice his first extensive experiments with the Negro as the comic butt, the minstrel stooge, the inane, foolish 'yassah' man of long-standing minstrel tradition.

Although Mark Twain would continue to explore this tradition of the black buffoon as scapegoat for white humour long after his experience in the West was over, Samuel Clemens reached the peak of his race prejudice during the Western years. Soon after his arrival in the East in 1867, as a potential member of the eastern establishment, as well as the son-in-law of a man who had been a leading conductor on the New York underground railway before the war and a public man of letters under pressure to re-evaluate some of his more extreme feelings about the Negro, Clemens in fact did begin to shift his emotional allegiance (the kind he valued most) to a partly reconstructed view of the black man. In this sense, then, the half-decade that Clemens spent in the Far West serves as a watershed period in his reaction to the Negro – a turning point that, within a year after his return to the East, would lead him to launch a new career of at least liberal lip service to the black race. □

The conclusion to the second essay develops this argument:

■ Even more, his growing attachment to the Langdon family during this period convinced Clemens that reform was not only desirable, but mandatory. Jervis Langdon, soon to be Clemens's father-in-law, had housed and shuttled runaway slaves through the New York under-ground, and had suffered a certain amount of social criticism for entertaining such abolitionists as William Lloyd Garrison, Wendell Phillips, Gerritt Smith, and Frederic Douglass in his home. Little wonder that when Langdon requested letters of reference regarding Clemens's past character and conduct, Clemens asked only strong Unionist and Republican friends in California and Nevada to write on his behalf.

Yet it would be hazardous to suggest that Clemens's somewhat altered attitudes toward Black men were grounded entirely on public expedience rather than private conviction. On the contrary, his exposure to men of wider intellectual horizons in Europe, the Middle East, and the Eastern states made it inevitable that he would revise some of his more outspoken racist views. The vacillatory, faltering, and incomplete nature of his reconstruction regarding the Negro during this period simply underscores the difficulty of such a conver-sion, not that a partial conversion was not taking place.

Still groping, still adjusting to the society in which he had volun-tarily encased himself, it is not surprising that Mark Twain's ability to render effective Black character portrayals still lagged somewhat behind Clemens's personal efforts to acquire a more tolerant attitude toward Negroes in general. That he failed to go even farther during this period probably speaks at least as much for the society and times in which he lived as for Clemens himself. □

Tom Sawyer may confirm Pettit's point about the difficulty even an enlightened Twain had in creating 'effective Black characters'. In this novel slavery itself, as Arlin Turner notes, is 'represented only by Jim, a "small coloured boy" who blends into the pleasantly hazy background'.[33] *Tom Sawyer* was never imagined as a powerful enough vehicle to carry the most divisive issue of Twain's personal life, and of the life of his nation. Nonetheless, the novel has a representative of another race to which enormous injustice has been done. Even in this nostalgic book, Twain engages with the complicating energies of his culture. Fantasies of the outcast indulged in Tom meet their desperate counterpart in the Ishmaelite Injun Joe, the son of mixed race and visible evidence of those acts of depredation against the Native American by which white society had established itself.

Injun Joe's contribution to *Tom Sawyer* renders banal Helen L. Harris's thesis that when Twain 'wrote of the native American he was unfailingly hostile'. According to Harris,

■ *The Adventures of Tom Sawyer* (1876) projected Twain's version of the native American to everyone, from the nineteenth century on, who read his immensely popular book. In the character Injun Joe, Twain demonstrated the typical Indian's treachery, murderousness, cowardice and depravity. The Welchman [sic] in the story pointed out to Huck the essential difference between an Indian and a white man as demonstrated by their attitudes toward mutilation as a form of revenge. A white man wouldn't do it but an Indian would.[34] □

Here it is simply assumed a character in a novel speaks for the author, and it is forgotten that Injun Joe is of mixed race.

Cynthia Griffin Wolff gets nearer to the heart of the matter. Observing that the society of St Petersburg is a 'matriarchy', she comments:

■ With no acceptable model of *'free'* adult masculinity available, Tom does his best to cope with the prevailing feminine system without being irretrievably contaminated by it. His principal recourse is an entire repertoire of games and pranks and superstitions, the unifying motif of which is a struggle for control. Control over his relationship with Aunt Polly is a major area of warfare. Thus the first scene in the book is but one type of behaviour that is repeated in ritual form throughout the book. Tom, caught with his hands in the jam jar – about to be switched!

> 'My! Look behind you, aunt!' The old lady whirled round, and snatched her skirts out of danger. The lad fled, on the instant, scrambled up the high board fence, and disappeared over it. His Aunt Polly stood surprised a moment, and then broke into a gentle laugh. 'Hang the boy. Can't I never learn anything? Ain't he played me tricks enough like that for me to be looking out for him by this time?'

Crawling out of his bedroom window at night is another type of such behaviour, not important because it permits this or that specific act, but significant as a general assertion of the right to govern his own comings and goings. Bartering is still another type of this behaviour. Trading for blue Bible coupons or tricking his playmates into painting the fence – these are superb inventions to win the prizes of a genteel society without ever genuinely submitting to it.

The logical continuation of such stratagems would be actual defiance: the rebellion of authentic adolescence to be followed by a manhood in which Tom and his peers might define the rules by which society is to be governed. But manhood never comes to Tom; anger and defiance remain disguised in the games of childhood.

Twain offers these pranks to us as if they were no more than humorous anecdotes; Aunt Polly is always more disposed to smile at them than to take them seriously. However, an acquiescence to the merely comic in this fiction will blind us to its darker side. A boy who seeks to control himself and his world so thoroughly is a boy deeply and constantly aware of danger – justifiably so, it would seem, for an ominous air of violence hangs over the entire tale. It erupts even into the apparently safe domestic sphere. . . .

Violence is everywhere in Tom's world. Escape to the island does not answer: random, pitiless destruction can find a frightened boy just as lightning, by chance, can blast a great sycamore to fall on the children's camp and signify that catastrophe is never far away.

Clearly, Tom is a major figure in the play of violence yet his part is not clear. Is he victim or perpetrator? Is the violence outside of him, or is it a cosmic reflection of something that is fundamental to his own nature?

His games, for example, have a most idiosyncratic quality; the rebellion and rage that never fully surface in his dealings with Aunt Polly and the other figures of authority in this matriarchal world find splendid ventilation in fantasy. Richly invigorated by his imagination, Tom can blend the elements of violence and control exactly to suit his fancy. Acquiescent to society's tenets in real life, in day-dreams Tom is always a rebel.[35] □

In Wolff's account Tom's rebellion becomes one more expression of that male desire for freedom from the matriarchy and from domesticity which is common in nineteenth century American literature. 'Manhood never comes to Tom', however, and in American literature generally the rebellion may lead nowhere. What is new in Wolff's piece is her seeing danger and violence in Tom's rebellion, and thereby associating Tom with Injun Joe:

■ Given the precarious balancing of control and violence in Tom's fantasies, we can easily comprehend his terrified fascination with Injun Joe's incursions into the 'safety' of St Petersburg. Accidentally witness to Injun Joe's murderous attack, Tom's first response is characteristic: he writes an oath in blood, pledging secrecy 'Huck Finn and Tom Sawyer swears they will keep mum about this and they wish they may Drop down dead in Their tracks if they ever tell and Rot.' It is an essentially 'literary' manoeuvre, and Tom's superstitious faith in its efficacy is of a piece with the 'rules' he has conned from books about outlaws. However, Injun Joe cannot easily be relegated to the realm of such villains. It is as if one element in Tom's fantasy world has torn loose and broken away from him, roaming restlessly – a ruthless predator – genuinely and mortally dangerous.

He has murdered a man, but perversely, he does not flee. Instead, he loiters about the town in disguise, waiting for the moment to arrive when he can take 'revenge.' Humiliated once by the Widow Douglas's husband (no longer available to the Indian's rage), Joe plans to work his will upon the surviving mate. 'Oh, don't kill her! Don't do that!' his nameless companion implores.

> 'Kill? Who said anything about killing? I would kill *him* if he was here; but not her. When you want to get revenge on a woman you don't kill her – bosh! you go for her looks. You slit her nostrils – you notch her ears like a sow!
>
> I'll tie her to the bed. If she bleeds to death, is that my fault? I'll not cry, if she does.'

It is almost a parody of Tom's concocted 'rules' for outlaws; even Injun Joe flinches from killing a woman. Sadistic torture (of a clearly sexual nature) is sufficient.

His grievance is twofold: against the absence of the man who would be his natural antagonist; and then against the woman who has inherited the man's property and authority. Seen in this light, his condition is not unlike the hero's. Tom, denied the example of mature men whom he might emulate, is left with no model to define an adult nature of his own. Tom, adrift in a matriarchal world – paying the continuous 'punishment' of guilt for the 'crime' of his resentment at genteel restraints, conceiving carefully measured fantasies within which to voice (and mime) his feelings. Injun Joe is Tom's shadow self, a potential for retrogression and destructiveness that cannot be permitted abroad.

Yet genuine vanquishment is no easy task. No other adult male plays so dominant a role in the novel as Injun Joe. Indeed, no other male's name save Huck's and Tom's is uttered so often. The only contender for adult masculine prominence is that other angry man, Mr Dobbin. But the schoolmaster's vicious instincts are, in the end, susceptible to control through humour: he can be humiliated and disarmed by means of a practical joke. After all is said and done, he is an 'acceptable' male, that is, a domesticated creature. The Indian, an outcast and a savage, is unpredictable; he may turn fury upon the villagers or act as ultimate executioner for Tom. When Tom's tentative literary gestures prove insufficient, desperate remedies are necessary: Twain invokes the ultimate adventure. Death. □

'Injun Joe is Tom's shadow self, a potential for retrogression and destructiveness that cannot be permitted abroad.' Wolff might have gone further with this arresting perception, which already develops Cox's reading. If Injun Joe is Tom's shadow-self, he is surely also Twain's, since Tom is a version of Twain.

Is it not some absolute longing for freedom, even if expressed violently, that Twain represses in himself in the death he contrives for Injun Joe? Developing her idea of death as the ultimate adventure, Wolff continues:

■ The triumph of 'temporary death' and the fulfilment of that universal fantasy – to attend one's own funeral and hear the tearful eulogies and then to parade boldly down the aisle (patently and impudently alive) – is the central event in the novel. The escapade is not without its trials: a terrible lonesomeness during the self-imposed banishment and a general sense of emptiness whenever Tom falls to 'gazing longingly across the wide river to where the village lay drowsing in the sun.' Yet the victory is more than worth the pain. Temporarily, at least, Tom's fondest ambitions for himself have come true. 'What a hero Tom was become, now! He did not go skipping and prancing, but moved with a dignified swagger as became a pirate who felt that the public eye was on him.' He has definitely become 'somebody' for a while – and he has achieved the identity entirely upon his own terms.

Yet this central miracle of resurrection is merely a rehearsal. Its results are not permanent, and Tom must once again submit to death and rebirth in order to dispatch the spectre of Injun Joe forever.

The escapade begins light-heartedly enough: a party and a picnic up river into the countryside. Yet this moderated excursion into wilderness turns nightmare in the depths of the cave. 'It was said that one might wander days and nights together through its intricate tangle of rifts and chasms, and never find the end of the cave. . . . No man "knew" the cave. That was an impossible thing.' Existing out of time, the cave is a remnant of man's prehistory – a dark and savage place, both fascinating and deadly. Once lost in the cave, Tom and Becky must face their elemental needs – hunger, thirst, and the horror, now quite real, of extinction. For Tom alone, an additional confrontation awaits: he stumbles upon Injun Joe, who has taken refuge in this uttermost region. □

Tom emerges triumphant from the cave:

■ Yet it is a hollow victory after all. Just as Tom must take on faith the pronouncement of his future as a 'great lawyer' or a 'great soldier' (having no first-hand information about these occupations), so we must accept the validity of his 'triumph.' The necessary condition for Tom's final peace of mind (and for his acquisition of the fortune) is the elimination of Injun Joe. And this event occurs quite accidentally. Taking the children's peril as a warning, the villagers have shut the big door to the cave and triple-bolted it, trapping Injun Joe inside. When the full consequences of the act are discovered, it is too late; the outcast has died. 'Injun Joe lay stretched upon the ground, dead, with his face close to the crack of the door . . . Tom was touched, for he knew by his own experience how this wretch had suffered. . . . Nevertheless he felt an abounding sense of relief and security, now.'

Tom's final identification with the savage, valid as it certainly is, gives the lie to the conclusion of this tale. What do they share? Something irrational and atavistic, something ineradicable in human nature. Anger, perhaps; violence, perhaps. Some unnamed, timeless element. . . . □

What Tom and Injun Joe share is what Twain and Injun Joe share. Twain ran away from the killing in the Civil War, but the imagination of violence is recurrent in his fiction. He is fascinated by figures, often authoritarian, who are freed from moral restraint and all the qualms of conscience, and who can thus cut through unending human complication with a simplifying violent act. 'The Facts Behind the Recent Carnival of Crime in Connecticut' (1876) illustrates this fascination already apparent in *The Innocents Abroad* (for example in the response to poor Arabs in chapter 51), and given powerful expression again in Colonel Sherburn in *Huckleberry Finn* and in Satan in *The Mysterious Stranger*. Part of its motivation, manifest in Injun Joe's case, is revenge for all feelings of impotence and futility.

Stuart Hutchinson develops the relationship between Injun Joe, Tom and Twain:

■ Tom can be the acceptable rebel in *Tom Sawyer*, because the violence, with which in other books Twain's imagination savaged the world, is villainized in Injun Joe. While Tom would be a Sir Galahad to a womankind whom the author himself can denigrate as 'sappy women' (Ch.34), Injun Joe has other desires:

When you want to get revenge on a woman you don't kill her – bosh! you go for her looks. You slit her nostrils – you notch her ears like a sow! (Ch.30)

Who can be surprised that Injun Joe, having designs of this nature, has been ostracised, jailed and 'horsewhipped' (Ch.30)? Yet the first cause of the *antagonism* between *Injun Joe* and St. Petersburg is never established. It is not clear, for example, who was originally in the wrong in the grudge Injun Joe bears against Dr. Robinson. Injun Joe tells the doctor:

> Five years ago you drove me away from your father's kitchen one night, when I come to ask for something to eat, and you said I warn't there for any good; and when I swore I'd get even with you if it took a hundred years, your father had me jailed for a vagrant. Did you think I'd forget? The Indian blood ain't in me for nothing. (Ch.9)[36] □

'Revenge on a woman'; how did Howells, apparently wanting to ensure a benign *Tom Sawyer,* overlook this extreme misogyny? How strong was such a passion in Twain himself, as he created all those versions of the self who, with other males, searched for freedom from all the entanglements of 'sappy women'? Alexander E. Jones reminds us that Twain worshipped his wife, Livy, 'as an example of ideal womanhood' and that she also became one of his mother substitutes:

■ Unconsciously however, he must have resented his wife's superior 'virtue',[37] no matter how proud of it he might seem on the conscious level of thought, because it would produce in him a profound sense of inferiority very damaging to his ego.[38] Therefore, as often happens in cases of masochism, he also engaged from time to time in acts which had mild sadistic overtones – a psychiatrist would call them examples of 'aggressive behaviour'. As Paine has said, 'He was continually doing such things as the "crippled coloured uncle" partly for the very joy of the performance, but partly, too, to disturb her serenity, to incur her reproof, to shiver her a little – "shock" would be too strong a word'.[39] To an observer such actions would seem to be 'teasing': and so they were. perhaps. But Van Wyck Brooks is also right when he senses subtler and less innocent motivation, when he pictures an unconscious self that 'barely discloses its claws' in the guise of playful tenderness.[40] According to modern psychiatric theory, not even the most passionate love of a man for a woman is free from a certain amount of hate or aggressiveness:[41] and in an individual like Mark Twain the cycle is complete: masochistic self-abasement gives way to sadistic behaviour, which in turn produces masochistic guilt. And thus there was set in motion a wheel of fire which spun steadily, causing new pain with each revolution and stopping only at Livy's death, if then. Characteristically, when Twain 'looked for the last time upon that dear face', he was 'full of remorse for things done and said in the 34 years of married life that hurt Livy's heart'.[42]

These alternating periods of aggression and remorse do *not* indicate that Mark Twain and his wife were unhappily married.

Actually, as Wecter has said, they 'fell deeply and physically in love with each other'. What Twain's behaviour does indicate is that the union was not free from psychic disturbance.[43] □

Jones's argument points to an obvious relationship between Injun Joe's sadism towards women and impulses in Twain himself. It is not surprising, therefore, that Twain, in Hutchinson's words, does not produce 'rational cause and effect explanation for Injun Joe':

■ The offspring of passions, which may well have been rapacious on the white side, his function is to serve as the author's and the town's bogeyman and scapegoat. Like Twain's other mysterious strangers, he undermines whatever security the townspeople have, whether it be religious belief, or assumptions about their own courage (Ch.11). Because *Tom Sawyer* cannot cope with Injun Joe's threat, Twain, as much as the townspeople, demonises him in order to exorcise him. To Tom and Twain, Injun Joe is what Orlick is to Pip and Dickens in *Great Expectations*. He is the estranged self destined to a desolate fate. Among Tom's fantasies of escape from St. Petersburg, the desire to 'join the Indians' (Ch.8) provides the only scenario native to America. 'Injun Joe infested all [Tom's] dreams' (Ch.25), because he is the nightmare of these fantasies of self-gratifying adventure. No wonder Tom feels 'an abounding sense of relief and security', as he stands over the dead body of Injun Joe. With the end of this 'bloody-minded outcast' (Ch.34) in the cave from which Tom escaped having got the girl, nightmare too can be thought to be at an end. □

In the role of 'mysterious stranger', Injun Joe joins a line of other characters, beginning in 'The Celebrated Jumping Frog of Calaveras County' (1867), through 'The Private History of a Campaign that Failed' (1885) and 'The Man that Corrupted Hadleyburg' (1899), and ending in *The Mysterious Stranger* itself. These figures disturb complacency and may poison all delight. They may also expose a heritage of guilt which is never to be escaped.

Hutchinson's case is that Twain did try to escape guilt in *Tom Sawyer*. Whereas in *Huckleberry Finn* we are implicated in the novel's irresolvable conflicts,

■ *Tom Sawyer*, by contrast, promotes a feeling that the reader can rise superior to St. Petersburg's simplicity. The author has left such a town behind, and the conclusion suggests that Tom Sawyer himself may well do so. As befits a book with a Preface inviting us to indulge, *Tom Sawyer* is delivered in Twain's least unsettled authorial voice. Just as he is sure of 'the reader' (Ch.1), so Tom is sure of St. Petersburg and is never happier than when he is winning its applause as its star turn. Author and central character have a confidence about audience approval which contrasts markedly with the wryness of the author and narrator of *Huckleberry Finn*. Everything in *Tom Sawyer* is contained within a conventional moral scheme, which not even Injun Joe, Tom's counterpart, is allowed to disturb. His kind of violent assertiveness has been attractive to Twain from the time of 'The Story of the Bad Little Boy'. In *Tom Sawyer* it is rendered safe and unproblematic by being villainized and eventually entombed.

At worst St. Petersburg is irksome or boring to Tom. In either case he can usually triumph over it, as in the famous scene when he white-washes the fence. To us, St. Petersburg is mostly amusing, notwithstanding Chapters 11 and 18, when the town verges on pro-viding material which in *Huckleberry Finn* will propel Huck into haunted flight. Even conscience, an incubus to several of Twain's fictional selves and especially to Huck, is easily appeased in *Tom Sawyer*. Whereas in other works it insidiously prompts responses which rarely have a hope of resolving the problems addressed, in Tom Sawyer it presses Tom to do achievable good things, such as the saving of Muff Potter at Potter's trial for the murder of Dr. Robinson. □

In 'The Facts Behind the Recent Carnival of Crime in Connecticut' the narrator kills his conscience. Thus freed from moral restraint he can wipe out his enemies and begin life anew. In *The Mysterious Stranger* Satan, who despises the moral sense, enacts similar desires. Conscience in Twain is a reminder of guilt and of our impotence to assuage it. Tom Sawyer, however, has a conscience he can eventually live with, just as he can eventually live with his community. He is a Gatsby who gets the girl. Hutchinson makes the analogy with Fitzgerald's novel as he com-ments on Twain's presentation of the manners and culture of a small provincial town:

■ St. Petersburg is created with an intimacy and directness rarely equalled by nineteenth century English novelists. With the notable exception of Hardy, they tend always to be reaching down to this kind of provinciality through the webs of their own higher culture.

Similarly uncondescending is Twain's treatment of the male adolescent's infatuation with a girl. It initiates what becomes a contin-uing achievement in American fiction. I am thinking of the scene shortly after Tom has first seen Becky Thatcher and has rescued a flower she has tossed over the fence:

He wandered far from the accustomed haunts of boys, and sought desolate places that were in harmony with his spirit. A log raft in the river invited him, and he seated himself on its outer edge and contemplated the dreary vastness of the stream, wishing, the while, that he could only be drowned, all at once and unconsciously, without undergoing the uncomfortable routine devised by nature. Then he thought of his flower. He got it out, rumpled and wilted, and it mightily increased his dismal felicity. He wondered if she would pity him if she knew? Would she cry, and wish that she had a right to put her arms around his neck and comfort him? Or would she turn coldly away like all the hollow world'? This picture brought such an agony of pleasurable suffering that he worked it over and over again in his mind and set it up in new and varied lights, till he wore it threadbare. At last he rose up sighing and departed in the darkness. (Ch.3)

As on several occasions in *Tom Sawyer*, the consciousness here attributed to Tom belongs to someone older than the 'small boy' we were introduced to in Chapter 1. It looks forward to Gatsby's recollections of Daisy in *The Great Gatsby*. In both books the seeming inwardness with the central character at moments like this is really an infusion of authorial subjectivity. Both Twain and Fitzgerald could as well be saying 'I' as 'he', even though Fitzgerald tries to counter his own identification with Gatsby by using the screen of Nick Carraway. Twain himself goes some way to objectifying Tom's sentimentality with phrases such as 'dismal felicity' and 'pleasurable suffering'. A couple of paragraphs later, this comic distancing of author from character will be broadened, when the American Romeo, lying under the window of his beloved, has water thrown over him. The distancing, however, is never a separation. Even the two phrases just quoted are an identification with the proposed typicality of Tom's condition in this kind of situation. Such is the identification, it might be argued that with respect to Tom and Becky *Tom Sawyer* enacts male adolescent wish-fulfilment, culminating in the resourceful and strong male rescuing the weak and helpless female from the cave in which they are both lost.

If Tom and Becky were to grow up together, it seems they would define each other in very conventional gender roles. In this connection, the conclusion to *Tom Sawyer* seems to offer Tom as a notable exception to several of nineteenth century American literature's other significant literary figures, including Huck. In contrast to their endless commitment to autonomy, whatever the torments of their loneliness and estrangement, Tom is finally left with great wealth, a good chance of marrying a top girl in his community, and the prospect of an influential place in the world:

Judge Thatcher hoped to see Tom a great lawyer or a great soldier some day. He said he meant to look to it that Tom should be admitted to the National Military Academy and afterward trained in the best law school in the country, in order that he might be ready for either career or both. (Ch.36)

Fifty years before Scott Fitzgerald, it seems that Twain writes of a Gatsby, but a Gatsby legitimised and likely to get his girl. Since Tom will never grow up, however, the above conclusion remains no more than a proposition. Tom thus matches Gatsby, who is himself killed before reaching fulfilment. The rewards and accommodations beckoning the hero will never be attained. Dispossession prevails, at least by implication, even in *Tom Sawyer*. There is a suggestion of kinship after all, not only with Twain's more radically unsettled accounts of American Ishmaels, but also with the Ishmaels in *Arthur Gordon Pym*, *The Scarlet Letter*, *Moby-Dick*, Whitman's 'I', Dickinson's 'I' and *The Portrait of a Lady*. □

The potential dispossession of Tom, realised in the actual dispossession of Injun Joe, is the counter-statement to the novel's self-indulgence. Its critique of the novel's governing mood ensures the novel's continuing resilience.

CHAPTER THREE

The Adventures of Huckleberry Finn: (1884–85): Dates of Composition and Contemporary Reviews

H UCKLEBERRY FINN was published in England in December 1884 and in America in February 1885. According to Walter Blair,[1]

■ Almost certainly Twain started his novel early in July 1876, and completed it slightly more than seven years later, as he himself testified shortly after each of these dates. On August 9 1876, he wrote William Dean Howells that 'a month ago' he 'began another boys' book – more to be working than anything else. I have written 400 pages of it – therefore it is nearly half done. It is Huck Finn's Autobiography. I like it only tolerably well, as far as I have got, and may possibly pigeon hole or burn the MS when it is done.'[2] On August 22 1883, Twain said that he had almost finished the book – 'haven't anything left to do, now, but revise,' – and on September 1 1883, when he wrote his English publisher, he said that he had 'just finished' it.[3] □

In his later book, *Mark Twain and Huck Finn*,[4] Blair reveals that when Twain first put the novel down at the end of the summer of 1876 he had reached the end of chapter 16, where the raft is run down by a steamboat. This is the most crucial break in the writing of *Huckleberry Finn*, since it bears on whether or not Twain intended to, or even could, develop the novel's plot as announced in the first paragraph of chapter 15. Moreover, there were other breaks in the writing. According to Blair (p.199), Twain wrote 'chapters XVII and XVIII between mid-October 1879, and mid-June 1880 . . . chapters XIX–XXI between mid-June 1880, and mid-June 1883, and . . . the rest of the novel . . . in the summer of 1883'. Another complication revealed by Blair (pp.346–7) is that the episodes dealing with Huck's and Jim's adventures on the *Walter Scott* and the arguments about King Solomon and the French language (chapters 12 to 14) were written at the same time as the account of Jim's rescue (chapters 32 to 43). In other words, the material of chapters 12 to 14, which has nothing to do with a serious bid for freedom, was written at the end but inserted immediately after Huck's and Jim's flight had begun. Finally, we learn from Blair (p.357) that it was Charles L. Webster, Twain's nephew and head of his publishing firm, who, seeing *Huckleberry Finn* in manuscript, suggested that the so-called raft chapter be removed. This material occurred in chapter 16, when Huck at Jim's suggestion visits a huge raft floating down the river and hears keelboat talk and tall-tales. Webster was concerned that *Huckleberry Finn* was so much longer than *Tom Sawyer*. Twain casually agreed to the excision. He was in any case using this raft material, often printed as an appendix to modern editions of *Huckleberry Finn*, in *Life on the Mississippi* (1883).

Blair (p.351) alludes to numerous other changes to the manuscript, some suggested by Twain's family and by Howells. We begin, however, with readings which take no account of *Huckleberry Finn*'s long gestation. Recently, our knowledge of the initial responses to the novel has been transformed by Victor Fischer. According to Fischer,[5]

■ *Adventures of Huckleberry Finn* was not ignored by American critics in the way or to the extent supposed, nor were the reviews that did appear in the United States as uniformly unfavourable or as ignorant of what Mark Twain had achieved as has been thought. More than twenty contemporary reviews and well over a hundred contemporary comments on the book have now been found, and more than that certainly appeared and may yet be found in American newspapers and magazines. Although this number is small when compared with the more than fifty reviews that greeted both *The Innocents Abroad* (1869) and *The Gilded Age* (1873), the modest size of the critical arena was not the result of timid critics, bad publicity, and subscription publishing: it can be traced almost wholly to the author himself. Although disapproval of subscription publishing and the bad publicity affected some contemporary reaction, they did so principally in Massachusetts. Critics in Boston and New York did deplore the book, and their attitudes to some extent influenced opinions expressed in other cities around the country. However, *Huck* was also well received and intelligently praised in New York, Connecticut, Georgia, California, and even Massachusetts. Moreover, the Concord Library ban, which drew out so many hostile comments on the book, was also well and repeatedly denounced by editors who had already reviewed the book favourably, or who took this opportunity to defend it for the first time.

Finally, although Mark Twain found the hostile reaction emanating from Boston disturbing, he also discovered that his book was selling very well. In fact, the intrinsic merits of the book combined with this large sale to unify its readers over the next ten years. By 1896, the Philadelphia *Public Ledger* could say, 'We are suspicious of the middle-aged person who has not read "Huckleberry Finn"; we envy the young person who has it still in store'.[6] □

Twain's own responsibility for 'the modest size of the critical arena' in which *Huckleberry Finn* was initially received derives in Fischer's words from 'relatively small number of review copies' he ordered to be sent out. He was afraid that press notices might hurt the book; then he changed his mind and tried to catch up on opportunities he had missed. The Concord Library Ban is one of the most famous, or infamous, episodes in American cultural history. Fischer's account of it is full and authoritative:

■ In mid-March 1885, just after the first newspaper reviews had appeared, *Huck Finn* became news once again when it was banned by the Concord Free Public Library in Massachusetts. Many editorials appeared in answer to this action: some were written for papers which had already reviewed the book and took the occasion to reassess it, but more were for papers which had not previously expressed an opinion, but did so now. On the whole, the papers that had reviewed the book favourably remained favourable. Those that had been critical – the New York *World* and the Boston papers – took the incident and Mark Twain's subsequent letter to the Concord Free Trade Club as an opportunity to criticise the author's character as well as his book. The negative reaction in Boston, in fact, was so strong and so widely publicised that it has been mistakenly represented as typifying the book's American reception.

When the Concord Library Committee – Edward W. Emerson, Henry M. Grout, George A. King, Reuben N. Rice, and James L. Whitney – decided not to circulate a copy of *Huck Finn* that had been purchased by the library, and made public their reasons, the Boston *Transcript* published a brief account of the action on 17 March, noting that the 'librarian and the other members of the committee' characterised the whole book as being 'more suited to the slums than to intelligent, respectable people'.[7] Fuller accounts, clearly from the same source as the *Transcript* story, appeared in the St Louis *Globe–Democrat* of 17 March and the *New York Herald* of 18 March. The *Globe–Democrat*, after noting the library's action, quoted the committee members at length, without comment:

Said one member of the committee: 'While I do not wish to state it as my opinion that the book is absolutely immoral in its tone, still it seems to me that it contains but very little humour, and that little is of a very coarse type. If it were not for the author's reputation the book would undoubtedly meet with severe criticism. I regard it as the veriest trash.' Another member says: 'I have examined the book and my objections to it are these: It deals with a series of adventures of a very low grade of morality: it is couched in the language of a rough ignorant dialect, and all through its pages there is a systematic use of bad grammar and employment of rough, coarse, inelegant expressions. It is also very irreverent. To sum up, the book is flippant and irreverent in its style. It deals with a series of experiences that are certainly not elevating. The whole book is of a class that is more profitable for the slums than it is for respectable people, and it is trash of the veriest sort.'[8]

The *Herald*, which also quoted the committee, was clearly amused by the ban:

The sage censors of the Concord public library have unanimously reached the conclusion that *Huckleberry Finn* is not the sort of reading matter for the knowledge seekers of a town which boasts the only 'summer school of philosophy' in the universe. They have accordingly banished it from the shelves of that institution.

The reasons which moved them to this action are weighty and to the point. One of the Library Committee, while not prepared to hazard the opinion that the book is 'absolutely immoral in its tone,' does not hesitate to declare that to him 'it seems to contain but very little humour.' Another committeeman perused the volume with great care and discovered than it was 'couched in the language of a rough ignorant dialect' and that 'all through its pages there is a systematic use of bad grammar and an employment of inelegant expressions.' The third member voted the book 'flippant' and 'trash of the veriest sort.' They all united in the verdict than 'it deals with a series of experiences that are certainly not elevating,' and voted that it could not be tolerated in the public library.

The committee very considerately explain the mystery of how this unworthy production happened to find its way into the collection under their charge. 'Knowing the author's reputation,' and presumably being familiar with the philosophic pages of *The Innocents Abroad, Roughing It, The Adventures of Tom Sawyer, The Jumping Frog, &.c.*, they deemed it 'totally unnecessary to make a very careful examination of *Huckleberry Finn* before sending it to Concord.' But the learned librarian, probably seizing upon it on its arrival to peruse it with eager zest, was 'not particularly pleased with it.' He promptly communicated his feelings to the committee, who at once proceeded to enter upon a critical reading of the suspected volume, with the results that are now laid before the public.[9]

News of the ban, often reported without editorial comment, spread immediately; appearing within two days in papers as far away as California. On 18 March the San Jose *Times–Mercury* noted that the 'Concord Public Library Committee has unanimously decided to exclude Mark Twain's new book.'[10] The following day, the Stockton *Evening Mail* printed a similar dispatch adding that the book was excluded 'as flippant, irreverent and trashy.'[11] Most papers, however, could not resist editorial comment. The Boston *Daily Globe* of 17 March used the occasion to mock not only the library committee but the town's reputation for obscure Transcendental thought:

> Members of the Concord public library committee have drawn the line on literature, and pronounced Mark Twain's *Huckleberry Finn* too 'coarse' for a place among the classic tomes that educate and edify the people. They do not pick out any particular passage, but just sit on the book in general. When Mark writes another book he should think of the Concord School of Philosophy and put a little more whenceness of the hereafter among his nowness of the here.[12]

The New York *World* of 18 March mistakenly thought the book had been 'repudiated by the Concord Public Schools,' but similarly joked that *Huck Finn* would be 'immensely popular with the Concord School of Philosophy, which will find in it no end of Henceness of the Which and Thingness of the Unknowable.'[13]

A few of the papers immediately called attention to the great advertising potential of the Concord ban, and implicit in their stories was a defence of the book. On 17 March the St. Louis *Post–Dispatch* wrote that the directors of the library had 'joined in the general scheme to advertise Mark Twain's new book *Huckleberry Finn*. They have placed it on the *Index Expurgatorius*, and this will compel every citizen of Concord to read the book in order to see why the guardians of his morals prohibited it. Concord keeps up its recent reputation of being the home of speculative philosophy and of practical nonsense.'[14] On 18 March the Hartford *Courant* was more explicit: 'The result [of the ban] will be that people in Concord will buy the book instead of drawing it from the library; and those who do will smile not only at the book but at the idea that it is not for respectable people.'[15]

On the same day; and in the same vein, the New York *Sun* wrote:

People who have watched the alarming rise and progress of the Concord Summer School of Philosophy will not be surprised that Mark Twain's delightful and healthful humour should be driven out of that unhappy village. Transcendentalism, even before it was second hand, and humour never got along with each other, and Concord has pampered its Over-soul at the expense of its understanding. In objecting to *Huckleberry Finn* as frivolous and what not, the authorities of the Concord Public Library have unconsciously and for the first time been humorous with a humour equal to that of Mr Clemens, who, by the way, ought to send them a small check in acknowledgement of the compliment and the advertising they have given him.[16]

Even the Concord newspaper, the *Freeman*, reprinted on 20 March the *mocking* story that had appeared in the Boston *Daily Globe* (and evidently the *Record*) on 17 March, and noted: 'Of course the committee are to be commended for their intentions, but, haven't they drawn the line a little inconsistently? As it is, however, the sale of the pr[o]scribed book has largely increased in Concord this week.'[17]

Mark Twain's initial reaction, perhaps after reading some of these earlier accounts was almost exultant. 'The Committee,' he wrote to Webster on 18 March, '. . . have given us a rattling tip-top puff which will go into every paper in the country. They have expelled *Huck* from their library as "trash & suitable only for the slums." – That will sell 25,000 copies for us, sure.'[18]

A number of other papers, however, particularly the Boston papers and the New York *World*, were more approving of the ban. ☐

Other incidents ensured publicity for *Huckleberry Finn*. According to Fischer,

■ On the three-month speaking tour that immediately preceded publication (November 1884–early February 1885), Mark Twain often read excerpts from it that were reviewed, quoted, and paraphrased by reporters. During this same period, he frequently gave interviews that were in part about his book.[19] Excerpts from it were syndicated in newspapers independently of the *Century*'s selections.[20] And just before (and after) publication, several much publicised crises involving the manufacture and sale of the book kept it in the news – not always favourably: 1) The obscene engraving. In late November 1884, Charles L. Webster (Mark Twain's nephew, recently appointed head of the author's publishing firm) was alerted to an engraving in the book that had been surreptitiously altered to make it obscene; the defective illustration had already been distributed in copies of the salesmen's prospectus, but not in copies of the book. On 27 November 1884, the New York *World* told the story of this embarrassment, and its account was reprinted and rehashed by other newspapers, particularly in New York City. 2) The Estes & Lauriat lawsuit. In December 1884, even before Mark Twain's agents had copies of the book in hand, the Boston booksellers Estes & Lauriat published a catalogue that advertised the book at a price below the standard agents' price. By 3 January 1885 Mark Twain had instituted a lawsuit, the progress of which was carefully followed in the press, with the Boston papers printing especially full accounts.[21] □

Blair[22] tells us that the illustration, from the novel's concluding episodes at the Phelps's, 'showed Uncle Silas with his pelvis thrust forward, Aunt Sally looking sideways at her spouse and grinning. The prankster with his awl or graver . . . drew a penis erectus at the appropriate place [in Uncle Silas's trousers].' The Estes & Lauriat lawsuit was Twain's attempt to get an injunction against Estes and Lauriat to prevent them selling *Huck Finn* at cut price. Fischer's conclusion is that,

■ Despite the evident distaste in some quarters for Mark Twain's commercial success, and despite his failure to secure an early favourable review 'by an authority,' *Huck Finn* was reviewed favourably and intelligently in a number of newspapers – in particular, the New York *Sun*, the Hartford *Courant*, *Post*, and *Times*, and the San Francisco *Chronicle*. It was also well defended by these and others in the discussion of the Concord Library ban. Within six years of publication, *Huck Finn* had left most of its detractors behind. In 1891, the year that the Webster company published the second edition, Andrew Lang pronounced it 'nothing less' than a 'masterpiece.'[23]

The following year, Brander Matthews called it a 'great book.' and quoted Robert Louis Stevenson's opinion that it was 'the strongest book which had appeared in our language in its decade.'[24] By the time the Harper edition came out in 1896 the personal attacks on Mark Twain that had interfered with the book's initial reception had been dispelled by the author's bankruptcy and subsequent efforts to pay off his debts. *Huck* was by then commonly called his best book.

In 1896, *Punch* published an appreciation of the book that called it 'a bit of the most genuine and incisive humour ever printed,' 'a great book,' and a 'Homeric book – for Homeric it is in the true sense, as no other English book is, that I know of.'[25] Later that year, the Harper edition was the occasion of almost universal approbation among the magazines that reviewed it, the one exception being *The Outlook*, which favourably reviewed the new plates and binding, but said ominously, 'Concerning the work of Mark Twain from the standpoint of American literature and humour, The Outlook will have more to say at a future day.'[26] *The Nation* noted that *Huck*'s 'power to interest and amuse has suffered nothing in the dozen years since it first saw the light.'[27] The *Critic* called it a 'masterpiece' which one read again 'with even more zest and appreciation than before,' and added:

> Our English cousins consider the book Mr Clemens's masterpiece, and The Athenaeum has declared it to be 'one of the six greatest books published in America.' It would probably be difficult to find many cultured people who have not read the story; but it would be even more difficult, we opine, to find many cultured people who do not desire to read it again.[28]

The Chicago *Dial* called Huck 'nearly, if not quite, the best of the books that we owe to Mr Clemens' (but did not add which of his books was thought better).[29] *The Independent* wrote:

> This is Mr Clemens's masterpiece. It is a book that will live, not as a great story; but as a truthful, tho somewhat exaggerated sketch, or series of sket[c]hes, of Southern life in the days of slavery. No other writer has equalled Mark Twain in making the absolute impression of what were the salient, distinguishing features of that life.[30]

Harper's Monthly used in its advertising copy the following statement from the Philadelphia *Ledger:*

> We are suspicious of the middle-aged person who has not read *Huckleberry Finn;* we envy the young person who has it still in store. . . . After the humour of the book has had its way then the pathos will be apparent, and later still will come the recognition of the value of these sketches as pictures of a civilisation now ended.[31]

In the same issue of *Harper's,* Laurence Hutton reviewed the new edition. saying that Huck 'is one of the most original and the most delightful juvenile creations of fiction,' and concluded:

> Happy the boy, of any age, who is to read *Huckleberry Finn* for the first time. It is safe to say that he will run the risk of prosecution in order to discover its motive; that he will take the chances of banishment rather than miss its moral; and, if he is anything of a mildly profane boy, 'he'll be shot if he don't find its plot.'[32]

In 1897, Brander Matthews compared Mark Twain with Cervantes 'in that he makes us laugh first and think afterwards.' Noting that three generations had laughed over *Don Quixote* 'before anybody suspected that it was more than a merely funny book,' he summed up:

> It is perhaps rather with the picaroon romances of Spain that *Huckleberry Finn* is to be compared than with the masterpiece of Cervantes; but I do not think it will be a century or take three generations before we Americans generally discover how great a book *Huckleberry Finn* really is, how keen its vision of character, how close its observation of life, how sound its philosophy.[33] □

Few other reviews of *Huckleberry Finn* need considering. The *Athenaeum* is clear about what kind of writer it believes Twain should be:

■ For some time past Mr Clemens has been carried away by the ambition of seriousness and fine writing. In *Huckleberry Finn* he returns to his right mind, and is again the Mark Twain of old time. It is such a book as he, and he only, could have written. It is meant for boys; but there are few men (we should hope) who, once they take it up, will not delight in it. It forms a companion or sequel, to *Tom Sawyer*. Huckleberry Finn, as everybody knows, is one of Tom's closest friends; and the present volume is a record of the adventures which befell him soon after the event which made him a person of property and brought Tom Sawyer's story to a becoming conclusion. They are of the most surprising and delightful kind imaginable.[34] □

Here the opening sentence returns to the question raised by our first review of *Tom Sawyer:* what claim on seriousness does Twain have? In the twentieth century the question perhaps goes in the opposite direction. James M. Cox[35] has argued that, by imposing seriousness on Twain, we fail to respond to Twain's humour and ignore its function of relieving guilt. The above reviewer, however, has read *Huckleberry Finn* very superficially. He sees no difference between it and *Tom Sawyer*.

The anonymous review in the English *Saturday Review*[36] was written by the American Brander Matthews, himself a creative writer and eventually professor of literature at Columbia. Matthews gets immediately to the essentials:

■ *Huckleberry Finn* is not an attempt to do *Tom Sawyer* over again. It is a story quite as unlike its predecessor as it is like. Although Huck Finn appeared first in the earlier book, and although Tom Sawyer reappears in the later, the scenes and the characters are otherwise wholly different. Above all, the atmosphere of the story is different. *Tom Sawyer* was a tale of boyish adventure in a village in Missouri, on the Mississippi river, and it was told by the author. *Huckleberry Finn* is autobiographic; it is a tale of boyish adventure along the Mississippi river told as it appeared to Huck Finn. There is not in *Huckleberry Finn* any one scene quite as funny as those in which Tom Sawyer gets his friends to whitewash the fence for him, and then uses the spoils thereby acquired to attain the highest situation of the Sunday school the next morning. Nor is there any distinction quite as thrilling as that awful moment in the cave when the boy and the girl are lost in the darkness, and when Tom Sawyer suddenly sees a human hand bearing a light, and then finds that the hand is the hand of Indian Joe, his one mortal enemy; we have always thought that the vision of the hand in the cave in *Tom Sawyer* is one of the very finest things in the literature of adventure since Robinson Crusoe first saw a single footprint in the sand of the seashore. But though *Huckleberry Finn* may not quite reach these two highest points of *Tom Sawyer* we incline to the opinion that the general level of the later story is perhaps higher than that of the earlier. For one thing, the skill with which the character of Huck Finn is maintained is marvellous. We see everything through his eyes – and they are his eyes and not a pair of Mark Twain's spectacles. And the comments on what he sees are his comments – the comments of an ignorant, superstitious, sharp, healthy boy, brought up as Huck Finn had been brought up; they are not speeches put into his mouth by the author. One of the most artistic things in the book – and that Mark Twain is a literary artist of a very high order all who have considered his later writings critically cannot but confess – one of the most artistic things in *Huckleberry Finn* is the sober self-restraint with which Mr Clemens lets Huck Finn set down, without any comment at all, scenes which would have afforded the ordinary writer matter for endless moral and political and sociological disquisition. We refer particularly to the account of the Grangerford–Shepherdson feud, and of the shooting of Boggs by Colonel Sherburn . . .

In *Tom Sawyer* we saw Huckleberry Finn from the outside; in the present volume we see him from the inside. He is almost as much a delight to any one who has been a boy as was Tom Sawyer. But only he or she who has been a boy can truly enjoy this record of his adventures, and of his sentiments and of his sayings. Old maids of either sex will wholly fail to understand him or to like him, or to see his significance and his value. Like Tom Sawyer, Huck Finn is a genuine boy; he is neither a girl in boy's clothes like many of the modern heroes of juvenile fiction, nor is he a 'little man,' a full-grown man cut down; he is a boy, just a boy, only a boy. □

Matthews' claim that 'Mark Twain is a literary artist of a very high order' contrasts markedly with those who want to see him only as a merchant of fun. Here it pertains especially to Twain's use of Huck as first-person narrator, the essential method of the novel with which all readings, if they are to be worth anything, must engage. Matthews is persuaded entirely by its consistency, a matter to be debated later, and he is impressed, rightly, by Huck's objectivity in the accounts of the Grangerford–Shepherdson feud and the killing of Boggs by Colonel Sherburn. This objectivity, the product of Twain's own 'sober self-restraint', has not always been appreciated by the moralising of the novel's twentieth century readers. Matthews himself is prevented from moralising by being alive to complication, especially in the qualities of the Grangerfords and the Shepherdsons. Interestingly, there is a suggestion at the beginning of the second paragraph that Huck is not gender-specific: 'only he or she who has been a boy can truly enjoy this record of his adventures'. The suggestion is not developed and may have more force for our own time than when it was made. It relates to the range of readers who can find themselves in Huck.

Matthews continues:

■ The contrast between Tom Sawyer, who is the child of respectable parents, decently brought up, and Huckleberry Finn, who is the child of the town drunkard, not brought up at all, is made distinct by a hundred artistic touches, not the least natural of which is Huck's constant reference to Tom as his ideal of what a boy should be. When Huck escapes from the cabin where his drunken and ruthless father had confined him, carefully manufacturing a mass of very circumstantial evidence to prove his own murder by robbers, he cannot help saying, 'I did wish Tom Sawyer was there. I knowed he would take an interest in this kind of business, and throw in the fancy touches. Nobody could spread himself like Tom Sawyer in such a thing as that.' Both boys have their full share of boyish imagination; and Tom Sawyer, being given no books, lets his imagination run on robbers and pirates and genies, with a perfect understanding with himself that, if you want to get fun out of this life, you must never hesitate to make believe very hard; and, with Tom's youth and health, he never finds it hard to make believe and to be a pirate at will, or to summon an attendant spirit, or to rescue a prisoner from the deepest dungeon 'neath the castle moat. But in Huck this imagination has turned to superstition; he is a walking repository of the juvenile folklore of the Mississippi Valley – a folklore partly traditional among the white settlers, but largely influenced by intimate association with the Negroes. When Huck was in his room at night all by himself waiting for the signal Tom Sawyer was to give him at midnight, he felt so lonesome he wished he was dead. □

In making the contrast between Tom's imagination and Huck's, it is noticeable that Matthews is more sympathetic towards Tom than modern readers are usually taught to be: 'if you want to get fun out of this life, you must never hesitate to make believe very hard'. This pronouncement associates Tom with Twain and suggests that Tom's motive for make-believe may be related to other extremes of behaviour recorded in the novel. It too may be a product of the unprecedented circumstances in which life on the banks of the Mississippi in the 1830s is being lived. Huck's particular forms of superstition are certainly the product of these circumstances and, in Matthews' view, especially the product of his 'intimate association with the Negroes'. Demonstrating the superstition, Matthews quotes from the penultimate paragraph of chapter 1, the first paragraph of chapter 32, and the account of the thunderstorm in chapter 9. His general, uncontroversial, point is that Tom has 'none of the feeling for nature which Huck Finn had caught during his numberless days and nights in the open air'. Where controversy does arise in the twentieth century is from white association of blacks with superstition. This matter will be discussed later, but it should be recognised that in *Huckleberry Finn* itself, what might be termed superstition, whether it be Jim's, Huck's or Pap's, has equal validity with all the other ways in the novel (especially Christianity) with which humankind deals with mystery.

Matthews concludes:

■ The romantic side of Tom Sawyer is shown in most delightfully humorous fashion in the account of his difficult devices to aid in the easy escape of Jim, a runaway negro. Jim is an admirably drawn character. There have been not a few fine and firm portraits of negroes in recent American fiction, of which Mr Cable's Bras-Coupe in the *Grandissimes* is perhaps the most vigorous, and Mr Harris's Mingo and Uncle Remus and Blue Dave are the most gentle. Jim is worthy to rank with these; and the essential simplicity and kindliness and generosity of the Southern negro have never been better shown than here by Mark Twain. Nor are Tom Sawyer and Huck Finn and Jim the only fresh and original figures in Mr Clemens's new book; on the contrary, there is scarcely a character of the many introduced who does not impress the reader at once as true to life – and therefore as new, for life is so varied that a portrait from life is sure to be as good as new. That Mr Clemens draws from life, and yet lifts his work from the domain of the photograph to the region of art, is evident to any one who will give his work the honest attention which it deserves . . . they are taken from life, no doubt, but they are so aptly chosen and so broadly drawn that they are quite as typical as they are actual. They have one great charm, all of them – they are not written about and about; they are not described and dissected and analysed; they appear and play their parts and disappear; and yet they leave a sharp impression of indubitable vitality and individuality. No one, we venture to say, who reads this book will readily forget the Duke and the King, a pair of as pleasant 'confidence operators' as one may meet in a day's journey, who leave the story in the most appropriate fashion, being clothed in tar and feathers and ridden on a rail. Of the more broadly humorous passages – and they abound – we have not left ourselves space to speak; they are to the full as funny as in any of Mark Twain's other books; and, perhaps, in no other book has the humorist shown so much artistic restraint, for there is in *Huckleberry Finn* no mere 'comic copy,' no straining after effect; one might almost say that there is no waste word in it, . . . □

Now we see why Matthews can be so easy on Tom Sawyer; he is not troubled by the treatment of Jim, not even in the final chapters. Jim, an example of 'the Southern negro', is given admirable qualities by Matthews, but they are not qualities to disturb whites. If his reading of the Jim in the novel is accurate, we may not be persuaded that Twain's portrayal of a fleeing slave is as 'true to life' as Matthews claims the other characters to be. We might expect more anger in Jim. Matthews' pronouncement, however, that the characters are 'not written about and about' conveys exactly their immediate dramatic vitality.

The reviewer in the London *Saturday Review* [37] finds in the Twain of *Huckleberry Finn* 'tenderness and melancholy, and an extraordinary sense of human limitations and contradictions'. In support of this perception, he cites especially 'the struggles of conscience of *Huckleberry Finn* about betraying the runaway negro'. Thomas Sergeant Perry, the last reviewer to be referred to, was a friend of Howells and of William and Henry James. *Century Magazine* had already published extracts from *Huckleberry Finn* in December 1884 and January and February 1885. Perry begins by contrasting the later novel with *Tom Sawyer*. He wonders whether the 'most marked fault [of *Tom Sawyer*] is not too strong adherence to conventional literary models':

■ This later book, *Huckleberry Finn*, has the great advantage of being written in autobiographical form. This secures a unity in the narration that is most valuable; every scene is given, not described; and the result is a vivid picture of Western life forty or fifty years ago. While *Tom Sawyer* is scarcely more than an apparently fortuitous collection of incidents, and its thread is one that has to do with murders, this story has a more intelligible plot. . . . [38] □

Perry ends:

■ What is inimitable, however, is the reflection of the whole varied series of adventures in the mind of the young scapegrace of a hero. His undying fertility of invention, his courage, his manliness in every trial, are an incarnation of the better side of the ruffianism that is one result of the independence of Americans, just as hypocrisy is one result of the English respect for civilisation. The total absence of morbidness in the book – for the *mal du siècle* has not yet reached Arkansas – gives it a genuine charm; and it is interesting to notice the art with which this is brought out. The best instance is perhaps to be found in the account of the feud between the Shepherdsons and the Grangerfords, which is described only as it would appear to a semi-civilised boy of fourteen, without the slightest condemnation or surprise, – either of which would be bad art, – and yet nothing more vivid can be imagined. That is the way that a story is best told, by telling it, and letting it go to the reader unaccompanied by sign-posts or directions how he shall understand it and profit by it. Life teaches its lessons by implication, non by didactic preaching; and literature is at its best when it is an imitation of life and not an excuse for instruction.

As to the humour of Mark Twain, it is scarcely necessary to speak. It lends vividness to every page. The little touch in *Tom Sawyer* where, after the murder of which Tom was an eye-witness, it seemed 'that his schoolmates would never get done holding inquests on dead cats and thus keeping the trouble present to his mind,' and that in the account of the spidery six-armed girl of Emmeline's picture in *Huckleberry Finn*, are in the author's happiest vein. Another admirable instance is to be seen in Huckleberry Finn's mixed feelings about rescuing Jim, the negro, from slavery. His perverted views regarding the unholiness of his actions are most instructive and amusing. It is possible to feel, however, that the fun in the long account of Tom Sawyer's artificial imitation of escapes from prison is somewhat forced; everywhere simplicity is a good rule, and while the account of the Southern *vendetta* is a masterpiece, the caricature of books of adventure leaves us cold. In one we have a bit of life; in the other Mark Twain is demolishing something that has no place in the book.

Yet the story is capital reading, and the reason of its great superiority to *Tom Sawyer* is than it is, for the most part, a consistent whole. If Mark Twain would follow his hero through manhood, he would condense a side of American life that, in a few years, will have to be delved out of newspapers, government reports, county histories, and misleading traditions by unsympathetic sociologists. □

'Hypocrisy is one result of the English respect for civilisation'? Is it true that the English settle for things and this settlement involves hypocrisy, whereas the American Huck Finn can settle for nothing and must therefore be committed to endless flight? Like Matthews, Perry praises the absence of comment about the Shepherdsons and the Grangerfords, and especially the general absence of condemnation and didacticism, two qualities ubiquitous in modern responses to the novel's characters and incidents. Finally and most significantly, Perry is the first to record doubts about what has remained among the most persistent of literary controversies, the ending of *Huckleberry Finn*.

CHAPTER FOUR

Huckleberry Finn: The Response of Creative Writers

IT IS a tribute to Twain's stature that well into the twentieth century he has continued to attract responses from major creative writers. Not surprisingly the concentration has been on *Huckleberry Finn* and usually its praise has been sung. Writing in the *London Bookman* Arnold Bennett, however, offers a fundamental criticism:

■ Episodically, both Huckleberry Finn and Tom Sawyer are magnificent, but as complete works of art they are of quite inferior quality. Mark Twain was always a divine amateur, and he never would or never could appreciate the fact (to which nearly all Anglo-Saxon writers are half or totally blind) that the most important thing in any work of art is its construction.[1] □

This judgement takes us back to the debate in Hamlin Hill's essay on 'The Composition and the Structure of *Tom Sawyer*'. It bears especially on what happens in *Huckleberry Finn* after Huck's struggle with his conscience and instinctive commitment to Jim in chapter 16. As we have discovered from Blair, it was at this point that Twain first abandoned the novel. When he eventually returned to it, several years later, he had apparently forgotten all about the Huck's and Jim's intended plan (announced in the first paragraph of chapter 15). Instead Huck and Jim continue southwards down the Mississippi, in a direction opposite to the one Jim needs to take if he is to find freedom. Bennett's view relates also to the ending of the novel, when Tom Sawyer returns and promotes fun and games irrelevant to the circumstances of a runaway slave. If we are looking for realistic plot and development in *Huckleberry Finn*, these eventualities may prove Bennett's case: Twain *was* 'a divine amateur', magnificent for an episode, but unable to construct a coherent whole. These will be recurrent issues in almost everything that follows.

T. S. Eliot read neither *Tom Sawyer* nor *Huckleberry Finn* till he was in middle age. Of the latter he writes that 'the opinion of my parents that it was a book unsuitable for boys left me, for most of my life, under the impression that it was a book suitable only for boys'. Having read it, he concluded that it was 'the only one of Mark Twain's various books which can be called a masterpiece':

■ *Tom Sawyer* did not prepare me for what I was to find its sequel to be. *Tom Sawyer* seems to me to be a boys' book and a very good one. The River and *the* Boy make their appearance in it; the narrative is good; and there is also a very good picture of society in a small mid-Western river town (for St Petersburg is more Western than Southern) a hundred years ago. But the point of view of the narrator is that of an adult observing a boy. And Tom is the ordinary boy, though of quicker wits, and livelier imagination, than most. Tom is, I suppose, very much the boy that Mark Twain had been: he is remembered and described as he seemed to his elders, rather than created. Huck Finn, on the other hand, is the boy that Mark Twain still was, at the time of writing his adventures. We look at Tom as the smiling adult does: Huck we do not look at – we see the world through his eyes. The two boys are not merely different types; they were brought into existence by different processes.

Tom Sawyer is an orphan. But he has his aunt; he has, as we learn later, other relatives; and he has the environment into which he fits. He is wholly a social being. When there is a secret band to be formed, it is Tom who organises it and prescribes the rules. Huck Finn is alone: there is no more solitary character in fiction. The fact that he has a father only emphasises his loneliness; and he views his father with a terrifying detachment. So we come to see Huck himself in the end as one of the permanent symbolic figures of fiction; not unworthy to take a place with Ulysses, Faust, Don Quixote, Don Juan, Hamlet and other great discoveries that man has made about himself.

It would seem that Mark Twain was a man who – perhaps like most of us – never became in all respects mature. We might even say that the adult side of him was boyish, and that only the boy in him, that was Huck Finn, was adult. As Tom Sawyer grown up, he wanted success and applause (Tom himself always needs an audience). He wanted prosperity, a happy domestic life of a conventional kind, universal approval, and fame. All of these things he obtained. As Huck Finn he was indifferent to all these things; and being composite of the two, Mark Twain both strove for them, and resented their violation of his integrity. Hence he became the humorist and even clown: with his gifts, a certain way to success, for everyone could enjoy his writings without the slightest feeling of discomfort, self-consciousness or self-criticism. And hence, on the other hand, his pessimism and misanthropy. To be a misanthrope is to be in some way divided; or it is a sign of an uneasy conscience. The pessimism which Mark Twain discharged into *The Man That Corrupted Hadleyburg* and *What is Man?* springs less from observation of society, than from his hatred of himself for allowing society to tempt and corrupt him and give him what he wanted. There is no wisdom in it.[2] □

Eliot's distinctions between *Tom Sawyer* and *Huckleberry Finn* are irrefutable. As for *Huckleberry Finn* itself, it is clear that he is reading it in a different way from Bennett. He is not looking for the same kind of realistic construction. Huck, in Eliot's eyes, is 'one of the permanent *symbolic* figures of fiction' [my emphasis], a character, in other words, having an essential significance greater than the immediate circumstances of his story. He is more than the character we see in the usual visual illustrations presenting his superficial appurtenances: straw hat, one suspender, ragged trousers and bare feet. 'There is no more solitary character in fiction', and this solitariness and 'loneliness' express for Eliot something integral to the human spirit and to the human condition. Huck is one of the great discoveries that man has made about himself. Paradoxically, this discovery derives from the boy Huck Finn in Twain which was the only part of him that was really adult; the ostensible adult Twain being actually the lesser figure, the boy Tom Sawyer. This Tom Sawyer Twain was the man of worldly success. He 'became the humorist and even the clown', but resented the 'violation of his integrity', an integrity realised in Huck Finn. This resentment is vented in Twain's final pessimism and misanthropy (see especially *The Mysterious Stranger*), both of which spring 'less from observation of society, than from his hatred of himself for allowing society to tempt and corrupt him and give him what he wanted'.

This diagnosis might help us to overcome doubts we might have about the narrow range of Twain's social observation as a basis for his polemics. D.H. Lawrence, in an essay written in 1927,[3] had also seen 'hate, a passionate, honourable hate' in Twain, but Eliot's general case about Twain's development owes much to Van Wyck Brooks' *The Ordeal of Mark Twain*.[4] Chapter 1 of this famous book tells us that the eventual bitterness of Twain

■ was the effect of a certain miscarriage in his creative life, a balked personality, an arrested development of which he was himself almost wholly unaware, but which for him destroyed the meaning of life. The spirit of the artist in him, like the genie at last released from the bottle, overspread in a gloomy vapour the mind it had never quite been able to possess. □

The spirit of the artist in Twain was frustrated because, in Brooks' view, he sold out to the Gilded Age. Chapter 6 tells us, 'he had adopted all the values and ideals of the bourgeois. Success, prestige, wealth had become his gods and the tribal customs of a nation of traders identical in his mind with the laws of the universe.' As Eliot sees it, he had become Tom Sawyer.

Bernard DeVoto[5] offers a passionate response to Brooks, seeking to demonstrate that the circumstances of Twain's upbringing were not as barren for the imagination as Brooks claims. Our involvement with this well-known controversy, however, is only for the purpose of giving some background to Eliot. Returning to the passage from Eliot quoted above and Eliot's attention to the 'boy' in Twain, it is worth raising the matter of Romanticism. The concept of uncorrupted child in harmony with nature is a commonplace of nineteenth century Romanticism, and in *Huckleberry Finn* itself it is given expression in the last paragraph of chapter 18 and the opening paragraphs of chapter 19. Fleeting as this experience in the novel is, it has none the less shaped many readings, as if Twain were somehow recommending life on the raft or whatever would be its equivalent. His involvement with Romanticism, however, always has a critical, realistic edge. In the particular instance a determining history, in the personages of the king and the duke, climbs on board the raft, returning Huck and Jim again to corrupted identities which will always shape their lives. Nor would we expect Eliot himself, given the positions of his poetry and prose, to endorse Romanticism. In fact the solitariness, the loneliness, the 'terrifying detachment', he stresses in Huck is the opposite of a harmony with anything.

'Repeated readings of the book', Eliot affirms later, 'only confirm and deepen one's admiration of the consistency and perfect adaptation of the writing. This is a style which at the period, whether in America or in England, was an innovation, a new discovery in the English language.' Moving on to Jim, he tells us: 'Huck in fact would be incomplete without Jim, who is almost as notable a creation as Huck himself. Huck is the passive observer of men and events, Jim the submissive sufferer from them; and they are equal in dignity'. This response pays no attention to Jim's particularities, not even to his basic condition as a runaway slave. It belongs to Eliot's intention to universalise *Huckleberry Finn*. The intention is valid and it needs someone of Eliot's authority to do it, but it produces a simpler novel than Twain wrote. Much of the complexity and tension of *Huckleberry Finn* derive from its engagement with the universal and the particular, with Jim as universal sufferer *and* runaway black slave in pre-Civil War America.

Eliot's universalising of the novel comes to a climax with his account of the river:

■ It is Huck who gives the book style. The River gives the book its form. But for the River, the book might be only a sequence of adventures with a happy ending. A river, a very big and powerful river, is the only natural force that can wholly determine the course of human peregrination. At sea, the wanderer may sail or be carried by winds and currents in one direction or another; a change of wind or tide may determine fortune. In the prairie, the direction of movement is more or less at the choice of the caravan; among mountains there will often be an alternative, a guess at the most likely pass. But the river with its strong, swift current is the dictator to the raft or to the steamboat. It is a treacherous and capricious dictator. At one season, it may move sluggishly in a channel so narrow that, encountering it for the first time at that point, one can hardly believe that it has travelled already for hundreds of miles, and has yet many hundreds of miles to go; at another season, it may obliterate the low Illinois shore to a horizon of water, while in its bed it runs with a speed such that no man or beast can survive in it. At such times, it carries down human bodies, cattle and houses. At least twice, at St Louis, the western and the eastern shores have been separated by the fall of bridges, until the designer of the great Eads Bridge devised a structure which could resist the floods. In my own childhood, it was not unusual for the spring freshet to interrupt railway travel; and then the traveller to the East had to take steamboat from the levee up to Alton, at a higher level on the Illinois shore, before he could begin his rail journey. The river is never wholly charitable; it changes its pace, it shifts its channel, unaccountably; it may suddenly efface a sandbar, and throw up another bar where before was navigable water.

It is the River that controls the voyage of Huck and Jim; that will not let them land at Cairo.

. . . Thus the River makes the book a great book. As with Conrad, we are continually reminded of the power and terror of Nature, and the isolation and feebleness of Man. Conrad remains always the European observer of the tropics, the white man's eye contemplating the Congo and its black gods. But Mark Twain is a native, and the River God is his God. It is as a native that he accepts the River God, and it is the subjection of Man that gives to Man his dignity. For without some kind of God, Man is not even very interesting.

Readers sometimes deplore the fact that the story descends to the level of *Tom Sawyer* from the moment that Tom himself re-appears. . . .

But it is right that the mood of the end of the book should bring us back to that of the beginning. Or, if this was not the right ending for the book, what ending would have been right?

In *Huckleberry Finn* Mark Twain wrote a much greater book than he could have known he was writing. Perhaps all great works of art mean much more than the author could have been aware of meaning: certainly, *Huckleberry Finn* is the one book of Mark Twain's which, as a whole, has this unconsciousness. So what seems to be the rightness, of reverting at the end of the book to the mood of *Tom Sawyer* was perhaps unconscious art. For Huckleberry Finn, neither a tragic nor a happy ending would be suitable. No worldly success or social satisfaction, no domestic consummation would be worthy of him; a tragic end also would reduce him to the level of those whom we pity. Huck Finn must come from nowhere and be bound for nowhere. His is not the independence of the typical or symbolic American Pioneer, but the independence of the vagabond. His existence questions the values of America as much as the values of Europe; he is as much an affront to the 'pioneer spirit' as he is to 'business enterprise'; he is in a state of nature as detached as the state of the saint. In a busy world, he represents the loafer; in an acquisitive and competitive world, he insists on living from hand to mouth. He could not be exhibited in any amorous encounters or engagements, in any of the juvenile affections which are appropriate to Tom Sawyer. He belongs neither to the Sunday School nor to the Reformatory. He has no beginning and no end. Hence, he can only disappear; and his disappearance can only be accomplished by bringing forward another performer to obscure the disappearance in a cloud of whimsicalities.

Like Huckleberry Finn, the River itself has no beginning or end. In its beginning, it is not yet the River; in its end, it is no longer the River. □

Eliot reminds us that the river is a mighty natural force, a dictator of directions. Whether or not we want to use the term God, it is the case that no great work of art is created without an engagement with forces remaining beyond human comprehension. With the river Twain has such a force, just as Melville has with the whale, Shakespeare with his storms and tempests and irrepressible human passions, Dickens with the contortions of urban life, Hardy with geological time. On this scale *Huckleberry Finn*, like the river itself, can have no beginning or end; or its end can only be its beginning. Since Huck's existence 'questions the values of America as much as the values of Europe', what was there to settle for? If there is, as Eliot suggests, an 'unconsciousness' about all great works of art in which the artist presumably gets to the essence of things, what but contrivance can ever provide an ending?

W. H. Auden establishes the Americanness of *Huckleberry Finn* by comparing it with *Oliver Twist*. 'The first thing maybe that strikes somebody who comes from England about [*Huckleberry Finn*] is the difference in nature and in the attitude towards nature.'[6] He suggests that to people in England nature is always:

■ in a sense, the mother or the wife: something with which you enter into a semi-personal relation. In the United States, nature is something much more savage; it is much more like – shall we say? – St George and the dragon. Nature is the dragon, against which St George proves his manhood. The trouble about that, of course, is that if you succeed in conquering the dragon, there is nothing you can do with the dragon except enslave it, so that there is always the danger with a wild and difficult climate of alternating, if you like, between respecting it as an enemy and exploiting it as a slave.

The second thing that will strike any European reader in reading *Huckleberry Finn* is the amazing stoicism of this little boy. Here he is, with a father who is a greater and more horrible monster than almost any I can think of in fiction, who very properly gets murdered later. He runs into every kind of danger; he observes a blood feud in which there is a terrible massacre, and he cannot even bear, as he writes afterwards, to think exactly what happened. Yet, in spite of all these things, which one would expect to reduce a small child either into becoming a criminal or a trembling nervous wreck, Huck takes them as Acts of God which pass away, and yet one side of this stoicism is an attitude towards time in which the immediate present is accepted as the immediate present; there is no reason to suppose that the future will be the same, and therefore it does not, perhaps, have to affect the future in the same kind of way as it does here.

Then, more interestingly, the European reader is puzzled by the nature of the moral decision that Huck takes. Here Huck is with his runaway slave, Jim, and he decides that he is not going to give Jim up, he is going to try to get him into safety. When I first read *Huckleberry Finn* as a boy, I took Huck's decision as being a sudden realisation, although he had grown up in a slave-owning community, that slavery was wrong. Therefore I completely failed to understand one of the most wonderful passages in the book, where Huck wrestles with his conscience. Here are two phrases. He says:

> I was trying to make my mouth say I would do the right thing and the clean thing, and go and write to that nigger's owner and tell where he was; but deep down inside I knowed it was a lie, and He knowed it. You can't pray a lie – I found that out.

He decides that he will save Jim. He says:

> I will go to work and steal Jim out of slavery again: and if I could think up anything worse, I would do that, too; because as long as I was in, and in for good, I might as well go the whole hog.

When I first read the book I took this to be abolitionist satire on Mark Twain's part. It is not that at all. What Huck does is a pure act of moral improvisation. What he decides tells him nothing about what he should do on other occasions, or what other people should do on other occasions; and here we come to a very profound difference between American and European culture. I believe that all Europeans, whatever their political opinions, whatever their religious creed, do believe in a doctrine of natural law of some kind. That is to say there are certain things about human nature, and about man as a historical creature, not only as a natural creature, which are eternally true. If a man is a conservative, he thinks that law has already been discovered. If he is a revolutionary he thinks he has just discovered it; nobody knew anything in the past, but now it is known. If he is a liberal, he thinks we know something about it and we shall gradually know more. But neither the conservative, nor the revolutionary, nor the liberal has really any doubt that a natural law exists.

It is very hard for an American to believe that there is anything in human nature that will not change. Americans are often called, and sometimes even believe themselves to be, liberal optimists who think that the world is gradually getting better and better; I do not really believe that is true, and I think the evidence of their literature is against it. One should say, rather, that deep down inside they think that all things pass: the evils we know will disappear, but so will the goods.

For that very reason you might say that America is a country of amateurs. Here is Huck who makes an essentially amateur moral decision. The distinction between an amateur and a professional, of course is not necessarily a matter of learning; an amateur might be a very learned person, but his knowledge would be, so to speak, the result of his own choice of reading and chance. □

Talk of St George and the dragon may remind us more of *Moby-Dick* than *Huckleberry Finn*. None the less, the river is as savage as the whale, and Auden is right to remind us of the different order of relationship an American writer may have with nature, when compared to English contemporaries. Shakespeare in *King Lear* of course is one reference point preventing the argument from getting too simplistic. Auden's reference to Huck's 'amazing stoicism' recalls Brander Matthews' response to his 'sober self-restraint' and Eliot's sense of his 'terrifying detachment'. The new ingredient is 'an attitude towards time in which the immediate present is accepted as the immediate present'. What other time but the present is there in *Huckleberry Finn*? The novel is written in the past tense, as if its experience is over and done with, but there is no sense that the narrator has arrived at a destination which is the result of his adventures and from which he is looking back. Despite the past tense, reading the novel is an engagement with a continuous present having an uncertain beginning and likely to have an inconclusive end. What happens in the present is not entailed by a past, nor does it entail a future. Americans, as Auden sees them, do not have the certainties which sustain the plotting of past, present and future: 'they think that all things pass: the evils we know will disappear, but so will the goods'. Huck, therefore, goes through no 'sudden realisation . . . that slavery [is] wrong'. His commitment to Jim is rather 'a pure act of moral improvisation', determining nothing.

All the above bears on the possibility of plotting in *Huckleberry Finn* and American literature generally. It renders banal Bennett's comment about construction. Twain is realising a culture in which the co-ordinates of coherence (beginning, middle and end) are elusive when they are not factitious. One of the outcomes of the realisation is the third point Auden has to make:

■ A third thing, . . . is that on reading *Huckleberry Finn* most Europeans will find the book emotionally very sad. Oliver Twist has been through all kinds of adventures; he has met people who have become his friends, and you feel they are going to be his friends for life. Huck has had a relationship with Jim much more intense than any that Oliver has known, and yet, at the end of the book, you know that they are going to part and never see each other again. There hangs, over the book a kind of sadness, as if freedom and love were incompatible. □

Is it the case that love itself belongs to compromising assumptions which in any event can never be relied on? Auden makes us aware again of the provisionality and lack of guaranteed prospect in *Huckleberry Finn*; if you build a village on the banks of the Mississippi, the waters will wash away its foundations.

The doom of living in an inescapable present is addressed by V. S. Pritchett:[7]

■ The peculiar power of American nostalgia is that it is not only harking back to something lost in the past, but suggests also the tragedy of a lost future. As Huck Finn and old Jim drift down the Mississippi from one horrifying little town to the next and hear the voices of men quietly swearing at one another across the water; as they pass the time of day with the scroungers, rogues, murderers, the lonely women, the frothing revivalists, the maundering boatmen and fantastic drunks of the river towns, we see the human wastage that is left in the wake of a great effort of the human will, the hopes frustrated, the idealism which has been whittled down to eccentricity and craft. These people are the price paid for building a new country. It is not, once you have faced it – which Dickens did not do in *Martin Chuzzlewit*, obsessed as he was with the negative pathos of the immigrant – it is not a disheartening spectacle; for the value of a native humour like Twain's is that it expresses a profound reality in human nature: the ability of man to adjust himself to circumstance and to live somehow.

Movement is one of the great consolers of human woe; movement, a sense of continual migration, is the history of America. This factor gives Twain's wonderful descriptions of the journey down the Mississippi their haunting overtone. His natural sensibility which is shown nowhere else in his writings and which is indeed vulgarly repressed in them is awakened: . . .

The subject of *Huckleberry Finn* is the comical but also brutal effect of an anarchic rebellion against civilisation and especially its traditions:

> I reckon I got to light out for the Territory ahead of the rest, because Aunt Sally she's going to adopt me and sivilize me and I can't stand it. I been there before.

Huck isn't interested in 'Moses and the Bulrushers' because Huck 'don't take no stock of dead people.' He garbles European history when he is discussing Kings with Jim, the negro. Whether Huck is the kind of boy who will grow up to build a new civilisation is doubtful. Tom Sawyer obviously would do so because he is imaginative. Huck never imagines anything except fears. Huck is 'low-down plain ornery', in trouble because of the way he was brought up with 'Pap.' He is a natural anarchist and bum. He can live without civilisation, depending on simple affections and workaday loyalties. He is the first of those typical American portraits of the underdog, which have culminated in the 'poor white' literature and Charlie Chaplin – an underdog who gets along on horse sense, so to speak. Romanticism, ideas, ideals, are repugnant to Huck.

Mark Twain obliges you to accept the boy as the humorous norm. Without him the violence of the book would be stark reporting of low life. For if this is a great comic book it is also a book of terror and brutality. □

Pritchett's remarkable observation about the 'peculiar power of American nostalgia', together with most of this extract, recalls Twain's hatred of the past, because it was 'so humiliating', referred to by Kazin in his comments on *Tom Sawyer*. Is it true that to renounce the past is also to renounce the future, since the past is the sum of all possible futures? Pritchett concentrates on *Huckleberry Finn*'s 'anarchic rebellion against civilisation and especially its traditions'. Again one thinks of the ending of the novel, where European culture returns if only in parodic form. In the desperation of Tom Sawyer's final intervention it is as if Twain is forced to recognise that attention to the old plots, however inadequate, must be paid; there may be no others.

Pritchett ends on what is now becoming a familiar note, the collapse of Twain after *Huckleberry Finn*:

■ Is *Huckleberry Finn* one of the great works of picaresque literature? It is, granting the limits of a boy's mind in the hero and the author, a comic masterpiece; but this limitation is important. It is not a book which grows spiritually, if we compare it to *Quixote, Dead Souls* or even *Pickwick*; and it is lacking in that civilised quality which you are bound to lose when you throw over civilisation – the quality of pity. One is left with the cruelty of American humour, a cruelty which is softened by the shrewd moralisings of the humorous Wards, the Will Rogers. And once Mark Twain passed this exquisite moment of his maturity, he went to bits in that morass of sentimentality, cynicism, melodrama and vulgarity which have damned him for the adult reader. I advise those who haven't read *Huckleberry Finn* since their school days to read it again. □

Pritchett's might be seen as an English point of view. For Scott Fitzgerald, Twain's non-European perspective is his strength:

■ Huckleberry Finn took the first journey *back*. He was the first to look *back* at the republic from the perspective of the West. His eyes were the first eyes that ever looked at us objectively that were not eyes from overseas. There were mountains at the frontier but he wanted more than mountains to look at with his restless eyes – he wanted to find out about men and how they lived together. And because he turned back we have him forever.[8] □

This was written for the centenary of Twain's birth in 1935. Its claim for Twain's western perspective is a familiar one, already eloquently made by Howells:

■ The West, when it began to put itself into literature, could do so without the sense, or the apparent sense, of any older or politer world outside of it; whereas the East was always looking fearfully over its shoulder at Europe, and anxious to account for itself as well as represent itself. No such anxiety as this entered Mark Twain's mind, and it is not claiming too much for the western influence upon American literature to say that the final liberation of the East from this anxiety is due to the West.[9] □

One understands the claims made for Twain's western perspective and its liberating, irreverent humour, but it needs to be remembered that Twain spent a sixth of his life in Europe[10] and that this experience would amount to an even larger proportion of his adult writing life. Howells' comment notwithstanding, Twain's books are full of the older European world, full of the tensions between it and the New World promise. As for Scott Fitzgerald, he seems still to be writing under the influence of *The Great Gatsby* and its mid-Western perspectives. He creates a sense of the American West looking back on what America has achieved. It is an idea which needs to be given more precision with respect to Twain.

Fitzgerald's contemporary, Hemingway, is responsible for a pronouncement which is now amongst the most famous of claims for Twain:

■ All modern American literature comes from one book by Mark Twain called *Huckleberry Finn*. If you read it you must stop where Nigger Jim is stolen from the boys. That is the real end. The rest is just cheating. But it's the best book we've had. All American writing comes from that. There was nothing before. There has been nothing as good since.[11] □

Even if one only thinks of 'before', this assertion writes off a lot of American literature: Cooper, Poe, Hawthorne, Melville, Whitman, Dickinson, Henry James! Like many other responses, it has no time for the ending of *Huckleberry Finn*. Also it makes some mistakes about the novel: the term 'Nigger Jim' does not appear in it, and Jim is stolen from Huck, not 'the boys'. But it is the writing in *Huckleberry Finn* that has impressed Hemingway's speaker, and familiarity with Hemingway's own prose tells us why. After the well-known modernist directives by Ezra Pound are taken into account ('Direct treatment of the "thing" whether subjective or objective'; 'To use absolutely no word that does not contribute to the presentation'), chapter 7 of *Huckleberry Finn* (paragraph beginning, 'I took the sack of corn meal . . .') shows us the non-theoretical, native American source of Hemingway. As with Hemingway's own prose, we have the direct recording of experience and that sense of contact with the real which is produced by bare nouns in simple sentences. Philip Rahv identified such prose as 'The Cult of Experience in American Writing.'[12] As he saw it, 'the typical American artist . . . all too often is so absorbed in experience that he is satisfied to let it "write its own ticket" – to carry him, that is, to its own chance or casual destination'. American writers in Rahv's view have a kind of fatalism in the face of experience; having recorded it, they do not know what to do with it. Unlike European writers, they do not know to what scheme of things it belongs. Again we return to the problem of structure in American literature. Rahv tends to treat the matter as if American writers are self-indulgent, or not up to the achievements of European writers. He pays insufficient attention to the fact that all European bets may be 'off' in American literature; or, at best, dubiously 'on'.

In one of his statements on Twain, William Faulkner criticises structure in Twain generally.[13] At the University of Mississippi in 1947 he was asked if the 'Great American Novel' had been written. His answer was that 'People will read *Huck Finn* for a long time. Twain has never really written a novel, however. His work is too loose. We'll assume that a novel has set rules. His work is a mass of stuff – just a series of events'. Faulkner is a very different novelist from Arnold Bennett, yet on this occasion he makes Bennett's kind of criticism of Twain. In Japan in 1955, by contrast, his view of Twain is more like Hemingway's:

■ Q: How do you think about Mark Twain, Mr. Faulkner?
FAULKNER: In my opinion, Mark Twain was the first truly American writer, and all of us since are his heirs. We descended from him. Before him the writers who were considered American were not, really; their tradition, their culture was European culture. It was only with Twain, Walt Whitman, there became a true indigenous American culture.
Q: Do you mean, Mark Twain was the first founder of your national literature?
FAULKNER: Yes, in a sense. Of course, Whitman was in chronology the first, but Whitman was an experimenter with the notion there might be an American literature. Twain was the first that grew up in the belief that there is an American literature and he found himself producing it. So I call him the father of American literature, though he is not the first one.[14] □

'All American literature comes from one book by Mark Twain called *Huckleberry Finn*.' Norman Mailer, himself a disciple of Hemingway, offers an ironic demonstration of Hemingway's point. A hundred years after it was published, he is reading the novel for the second time:

■ A suspicion immediately arises. Mark Twain is doing the kind of writing only Hemingway can do better. Evidently, we must take a look! May I say it helps to have read *Huckleberry Finn* so long ago that it feels brand-new on picking it up again. Perhaps I was 11 when I saw it last, maybe 13, but now I only remember that I came to it after *Tom Sawyer* and was disappointed. I couldn't really follow *The Adventures of Huckleberry Finn*. The character of Tom Sawyer whom I had liked so much in the first book was altered, and did not seem nice any more. Huckleberry Finn was altogether beyond me.

Later, I recollect being surprised by the high regard nearly everyone who taught American Lit. lavished upon the text, but that didn't bring me back to it. Obviously, I was waiting for an assignment from *The New York Times*.

Let me offer assurances. It may have been worth the wait. I suppose I am the 10-millionth reader to say that *Huckleberry Finn* is an extraordinary work. Indeed, for all I know, it is a great novel. Flawed, quirky, uneven, not above taking cheap shots and cashing far too many checks (it is rarely above milking its humour) – all the same, what a book we have here! I had the most curious sense of excitement. After a while, I understood my peculiar frame of attention. The book was so up-to-date! I was not reading a classic author so much as look-ing at a new work sent to me in galleys by a publisher. It was as if it had arrived within one of those rare letters which says, 'We won't make this claim often but do think we have an extraordinary first novel to send out.' So it was like reading *From Here to Eternity* in galleys, back in 1950, or *Lie Down in Darkness*, *Catch-22* or *The World According to Garp* (which reads like a fabulous first novel). You kept being alternately delighted, surprised, annoyed, competitive, critical and finally excited. A new writer had moved onto the block. He could be a potential friend or enemy but he most certainly was talented.

That was how it felt to read *Huckleberry Finn* a second time. I kept resisting the context until I finally surrendered. One always does surrender sooner or later to a book within a strong magnetic field. I felt as if I held the work of a young writer about 30 or 35, a prodi-giously talented fellow from the Midwest, from Missouri probably, who had had the audacity to write a historical novel about the Mississippi as it might have been a century and a half ago, and this young writer had managed to give us a circus of fictional virtuosities. In nearly every chapter new and remarkable characters bounded out from the printed page as if it were a tarmac on which they could per-form their leaps. The author's confidence seemed so complete that he could deal with every kind of man or woman God ever gave to the middle of America. Jail-house drunks like Huck Finn's father take their bow, full of the raunchy violence that even gets into the smell of clothing. Gentlemen and river rats, young, attractive girls full of grit and 'sand,' and strong old ladies with aphorisms clicking like knitting needles, fools and confidence men – what a cornucopia of rabble and gentry inhabit the author's river banks.

It would be superb stuff if only the writer did not keep giving away the fact that he was a modern young American working in 1984. His anachronisms were not so much in the historical facts – those seemed accurate enough – but the point of view was too contem-porary. The scenes might succeed – say it again, this young writer was talented! – but he kept betraying his literary influences. The author of

The Adventures of Huckleberry Finn had obviously been taught a lot by such major writers as Sinclair Lewis, John Dos Passos and John Steinbeck; he had certainly lifted from Faulkner and the mad tone Faulkner could achieve when writing about maniacal men feuding in deep swamps; he had also absorbed much of what Vonnegut and Heller could teach about the resilience of irony. If he had a surer feel for the picaresque than Saul Bellow in *Augie March*, still he felt derivative of that work. In places one could swear he had memorised *The Catcher in the Rye*, and he probably dipped into *Deliverance* and *Why Are We in Vietnam?* He might even have studied the mannerisms of movie stars. You could feel traces of John Wayne, Victor McLaglen and Burt Reynolds in his pages. The author had doubtless digested many a Hollywood comedy on small-town life. His instinct for life in hamlets on the Mississippi before the Civil War was as sharp as it was farcical and couldn't be more commercial.

No matter. With talent as large as this, one could forgive the obvious eye for success. Many a large talent has to go through large borrowings in order to find his own style, and a lust for popular success while dangerous to serious writing is not necessarily fatal. Yes, one could accept the pilferings from other writers, given the scope of this work, the brilliance of the concept – to catch rural America by a trip on a raft down a great river![15] □

Who better to speak for the modernity of *Huckleberry Finn* than Mailer, himself so enmeshed in the warp and woof of mid-twentieth century American culture? At the end of his piece he moves through a tribute to Twain's presentation of the river (recalling Eliot) and gets to the essential matter of slavery, with which few critics so far have engaged:

■ Few works of literature can be so luminous without the presence of some majestic symbol. In *Huckleberry Finn* we are presented (given the possible exception of Anna Livia Plurabelle) with the best river ever to flow through a novel, our own Mississippi, and in the voyage down those waters of Huck Finn and a runaway slave on their raft, we are held in the thrall of the river. Larger than a character, the river is a manifest presence, a demiurge to support the man and the boy, a deity to betray them, feed them, all but drown them, fling them apart, float them back together. The river winds like a fugue through the marrow of the true narrative which is nothing less than the ongoing relation between Huck and the runaway slave, this Nigger Jim whose name embodies the very stuff of the slave system itself – his name is not Jim but Nigger Jim. The growth of love and knowledge between the runaway white and the runaway black is a relation equal to the relation of the men to the river for it is also full of betrayal and nourishment, separation and return. So it manages to touch that last fine nerve of the heart where compassion and irony speak to one another and thereby give a good turn to our inmost protected emotions.

Reading *Huckleberry Finn* one comes to realise all over again that the near-burned-out, throttled, hate-filled dying affair between whites and blacks is still our great national love affair. and woe to us if it ends in detestation and mutual misery. Riding the current of this novel, we are back in that happy time when the love affair was new and all seemed possible. How rich is the recollection of that emotion! What else is greatness but the indestructible wealth it leaves in the mind's recollection after hope has soured and passions are spent? It is always the hope of democracy that our wealth will be there to spend again, and the ongoing treasure of *Huckleberry Finn* is that it frees us to think of democracy and its sublime, terrifying premise: let the passions and cupidities and dreams and kinks and ideals and greed and hopes and foul corruptions of all men and women have their day and the world will still be better off, for there is more good than bad in the sum of us and our workings. Mark Twain, whole embodiment of that democratic human, understood the premise in every turn of his pen, and how he tested it, how he twisted and tantalised and tested it until we are weak all over again with our love for the idea. □

It may be easier to be pessimistic than optimistic. Mailer at any rate is one of the few critics finding hope in *Huckleberry Finn*. For him the book is an ultimate testing and maintenance of the democratic premise, which is surely the only American dream that matters. At the heart of this premise is racial harmony, 'our great national love affair' 'between whites and blacks'. 'Hate-filled' and 'dying', when Mailer is writing, this affair, with all its promise, is momentarily realised between Huck and Jim, presumably in such paragraphs as those at the beginning of chapter 19. Such moments, amid all the corruptions, reassure: 'there is more good than bad in the sum of us and our workings.' That had better be true. At the same time, it needs recognising that when Mailer is writing the above piece, there is a lot more to American racial inter-involvement than white and black. In Mailer's reading *Huckleberry Finn* is in danger of being exploited in a sentimental racial debate which is too exclusive of other colours.

John Barth finds in *Huckleberry Finn* 'a tapping of some kind of mythic well that is larger than actual sentences':

■ There are images in fiction that haunt my imagination, so much so that I even keep a little list of them. Foremost among them are: Odysseus trying to get home: Scheherazade telling her stories: Don Quixote riding with Sancho across La Mancha; and Huckleberry Finn floating down that river. I would love one day, without aspiring to include myself in that biggest of leagues, to come up with a similar image, one that was as much larger than the book in which it appeared as those images are larger than the stories in which they appear.

I love language, and I really believe that Huck's language, Huck's voice, is as much a substance in that novel as the image of Huck and Jim drifting down the Mississippi. But an old poet and a former teacher of mine here at Johns Hopkins once warned me: no actual book could possibly live up to the magnitude of that image of Don Quixote and Sancho as it works on our imaginations, all of us, even before we read the book. I think that's an accurate remark about *Don Quixote*. There are certain images that have mythopoetic voltage, that really are larger than the text, however magnificent the text might be. Gregor Samsa's cockroach is one of those images; Moby-Dick is another. Leslie Fiedler talks about this sort of thing – although I suppose you could say that's his 'bag' – but what we're all addressing is a tapping of some kind of mythic well that is larger than actual sentences. I don't agree with Fiedler when he suggests that what's really important in literature is what you remember when you've forgotten all the words. But, to say it more accurately, and certainly he said it this way too, an index of the mythic element in fiction may be what you remember when you've forgotten all the words. It's also that aspect of the story that could be most easily translated into another medium without loss.[16] □

Another way of putting this is to think of the continuing 'afterlife' of all great works of literature during which so much accretes to a Hamlet and to a Huck and a Jim. Distinguishing the meretricious from the meritorious accretions, as we read again and again the only words in which these figures exist, is criticism's most challenging task.

Booker T. Washington provides our first black response to *Huckleberry Finn*. Writing in tribute to Twain in the year of Twain's death, Washington tells us:

■ It was my privilege to know the late Samuel L. Clemens for a number of years. The first time I met him was at his home in Hartford. Later I met him several times at his home in New York City and at the Lotus Club. It may be I became attached to Mr Clemens all the more strongly because both of us were born in the South. He had the Southern temperament, and most that he has written has the flavour of the South in it. His interest in the negro race is perhaps expressed best in one of his most delightful stories, *Huckleberry Finn*. In this, which contains many pictures of Southern life as it was fifty or sixty years ago, there is a poor, ignorant negro boy who accompanies the heroes of the story, Huckleberry Finn and Tom Sawyer, on a long journey down the Mississippi on a raft.

It is possible the ordinary reader of this story has been so absorbed in the adventures of the two white boys that he did not think much about the part that 'Jim' – which was, as I remember, the name of the coloured boy – played in all these adventures. I do not believe any one can read this story closely, however, without becoming aware of the deep sympathy of the author in 'Jim.' In fact, before one gets through within the book, one cannot fail to observe that in some way or other the author without making any comment and without going out of his way, has somehow succeeded in making his readers feel a genuine respect for 'Jim,' in spite of the ignorance he displays. I cannot help feeling that in this character Mark Twain has, perhaps unconsciously, exhibited his sympathy and interest in the masses of the negro people.[17] □

When he wrote this piece, Washington, author of *Up From Slavery* (1901), and the principal force behind the Tuskegee Institute which offered education to black men and women, had become the most influential figure in race relations in the United States. The non-militancy of his programme of peaceful co-existence, implicit in the above passage, has been much criticised in the later twentieth century. One wonders how long it was since he had read *Huckleberry Finn* and how he uses the term 'boy' of Jim. If he seems too grateful, however, for Twain 'making his readers feel a genuine respect for "Jim"' it should be remembered that 'between 1885 and 1910 approximately 3,500 blacks were lynched in America and that most southern states had by this time disenfranchised blacks'.[18]

Ralph Ellison has made several pronouncements about Twain and *Huckleberry Finn*, notably in 'The Seer and the Seen', 1946 and 'Change the Joke and Slip the Yoke', 1958.[19] In the first essay he argues that

■ Huckleberry Finn knew, as did Mark Twain, that Jim was not only a slave but a human being, a man who in some ways was to be envied, and who expressed his essential humanity in his desire for freedom, his will to possess his own labour, in his loyalty and capacity for friendship and in his love for his wife and child. Yet Twain, though guilty of the sentimentality common to humorists, does not idealise the slave. Jim is drawn in all his ignorance and superstition, with his good traits and his bad. He, like all men, is ambiguous, limited in circumstance but not in possibility. And it will be noted that when Huck makes his decision he identifies himself with Jim and accepts the judgement of his super-ego – that internalised representative of the community – that his action is evil. Like Prometheus, who for mankind stole fire from the gods, he embraces the evil implicit in his act in order to affirm his belief in humanity. Jim, therefore, is not simply a slave, he is a symbol of humanity, and in freeing Jim, Huck makes a bid to free himself of the conventionalised evil taken for civilisation by the town . . .

Huck Finn's acceptance of the evil implicit in his 'emancipation' of Jim represents Twain's acceptance of his personal responsibility in the condition of society. This was the tragic face behind his comic mask.

But by the twentieth century this attitude of tragic responsibility had disappeared from our literature along with that broad conception of democracy which vitalised the work of our greatest writers. After Twain's compelling image of black and white fraternity the Negro generally disappears from fiction as a rounded human being. And if already in Twain's time a novel which would include all men could not escape being banned from public libraries, his great drama of inter-racial fraternity had become, by our day for most Americans at least, an amusing boy's story and nothing more. ☐

At the end of this quotation Ellison is referring to the Concord Library ban and supporting Leslie Fiedler's long held, though more generalised and more dubious, position that 'the great works of American fiction are notoriously at home in the children's section of the library'.[20] Presumably, it is in the work of white writers that, after Twain, 'the Negro generally disappears from fiction as a rounded human being'. 'Tragic face behind his comic mask' is exactly right for some moments of Twain's relationship to Huck, though Ellison himself is close to losing this relationship by imputing too much consciousness to Huck and reading Huck as Auden says he used to read him. His identification of Jim as 'a symbol of humanity' is especially interesting in the light of his later essay:

■ It is not at all odd that this black-faced figure of white fun is for Negroes a symbol of everything they rejected in the white man's thinking about race, in themselves and in their own group. When he appears, for example, in the guise of Nigger Jim, the Negro is made uncomfortable. Writing at a time when the black-faced minstrel was still popular, and shortly after a war which left even the abolitionists weary of those problems associated with the Negro, Twain fitted Jim into the outlines of the minstrel tradition, and it is from behind this stereotype mask that we see Jim's dignity and human capacity – and Twain's complexity – emerge. Yet it is his source in this same tradition which creates that ambivalence between his identification as an adult and parent and his 'boyish' naivete, and which by contrast makes

Huck, with his street-sparrow sophistication, seem more adult. Certainly it upsets a Negro reader, and it offers a less psycho-analytical explanation of the discomfort which lay behind Leslie Fiedler's thesis concerning the relation of Jim and Huck in his essay 'Come Back to the Raft Ag'in, Huck Honey!'

A glance at a more recent fictional encounter between a Negro adult and a white boy, that of Lucas Beauchamp and Chuck Mallison in Faulkner's *Intruder in The Dust* will reinforce my point. For all the racial and caste differences between them, Lucas holds the ascendancy in his mature dignity over the youthful Mallison and refuses to lower himself in the comic duel of status forced on him by the white boy whose life he has saved. Faulkner was free to reject the confusion between manhood and the Negro's caste status which is sanctioned by white Southern tradition, but Twain, standing closer to the Reconstruction and to the oral tradition, was not so free of the white dictum that Negro males must be treated either as boys or 'uncles' – never as men. Jim's friendship for Huck comes across as that of a boy for another boy rather than as the friendship of an adult for a junior; thus there is implicit in it not only a violation of the manners sanctioned by society for relations between Negroes and whites. there is a violation of our conception of adult maleness.

In Jim the extremes of the private and the public come to focus, and before our eyes an 'archetypal' figure gives way before the realism implicit in the form of the novel. Here we have, I believe, an explanation in the novel's own terms of that ambiguity which bothered Fiedler; Fiedler was accused of mere sensationalism when he named the friendship homosexual, yet I believe him so profoundly disturbed by the manner in which the deep dichotomies symbolised by blackness and whiteness are resolved that, forgetting to look at the specific form of the novel, he leaped squarely into the middle of that tangle of symbolism which he is dedicated to unsnarling, and yelled out his most terrifying name for chaos. Other things being equal, he might have called it 'rape,' 'incest,' 'parricide' or – 'miscegenation.' It is ironic that what to a Negro appears to be a lost fall in Twain's otherwise successful wrestle with the ambiguous figure in black face is viewed by a critic as a symbolic loss of sexual identity. Surely for literature there is some rare richness here. . . .

I use folklore in my work not because I am Negro, but because writers like Eliot and Joyce made me conscious of the literary value of my folk inheritance. My cultural background, like that of most Americans, is dual (my middle name, sadly enough, is Waldo). I knew the trickster Ulysses just as early as I knew the wily rabbit of Negro American lore, and I could easily imagine myself a pint-sized Ulysses but hardly a rabbit, no matter how human and resourceful or Negro.

And a little later I could imagine myself as Huck Finn (I so nicknamed my brother) but not, though I racially identified with him, as Nigger Jim, who struck me as a white man's inadequate portrait of a slave. □

Here Ellison voices that fundamental sense of offensiveness experienced by black readers especially over some aspects of the characterisation of Jim, notably those derived from 'the minstrel tradition'. Faulkner's fans might have wanted to counter Ellison's earlier essay by citing Faulkner as a successful creator of rounded black characters. Now they get support from Ellison himself. The last words of the above quotation are, however, the ones that stay in the mind. It tells us much about the possibilities of response to Jim that a black novelist who has already found him 'a symbol of humanity' should also insist that he is 'a white man's inadequate portrait of a slave'.

Twain and *Huckleberry Finn* re-emerge again in Ellison's 'What America Would Be Like Without Blacks'.[21] Referring to 'the spoken idiom of Negro Americans' Ellison argues that

■ its flexibility, its musicality, its rhythms, freewheeling diction, and metaphors, as projected in Negro American folklore, were absorbed by the creators of our great nineteenth-century literature even when the majority of blacks were still enslaved. Mark Twain celebrated it in the prose of *Huckleberry Finn*; without the presence of blacks, the book could not have been written. No Huck and Jim, no American novel as we know it. □

What becomes a general thesis about the unacknowledged contribution of blacks to American culture is developed later by Toni Morrison.[22] She argues in her Preface that 'the readers of virtually all of American fiction have been positioned as white'. Moreover, 'living in a nation of people who *decided* that their world view would combine agendas for individual freedom and mechanisms for devastating racial oppression presents a singular landscape for a writer'. Twain's realisation of these agendas is presented in chapter 2 in Morrison's reading of *Huckleberry Finn*:

■ On this young but street-smart innocent, Huck, who is virginally uncorrupted by bourgeois yearnings, fury, and helplessness, Mark Twain inscribes a critique of slavery and the pretensions of the would-be middle class, a resistance to the loss of Eden and the difficulty of becoming a social individual. The agency, however, for Huck's struggle is the nigger Jim, and it is absolutely necessary (for reasons I tried to illuminate earlier) that the term nigger be inextricable from Huck's deliberations about who and what he himself is – or, more precisely, is not. The major controversies about the greatness or near greatness of

Huckleberry Finn as an American (or even 'world') novel exist as controversies because they forgo a close examination of the interdependence of slavery and freedom, of Huck's growth and Jim's serviceability within it, and even of Mark Twain's inability to continue, to explore the journey into free territory. . . .

The critical controversy has focused on the collapse of the so-called fatal ending of the novel. It has been suggested that the ending is a brilliant finesse that returns Tom Sawyer to the centre stage where he should be. Or it is a brilliant play on the dangers and limitations of romance. Or it is a sad and confused ending to the book of an author who, after a long blocked period, lost narrative direction; who changed the serious adult focus back to a child's story out of disgust. Or the ending is a valuable learning experience for Jim and Huck for which we and they should be grateful. What is not stressed is that there is no way, given the confines of the novel, for Huck to mature into a moral human being in America without Jim. To let Jim go free, to let him enter the mouth of the Ohio River and pass into free territory, would be to abandon the whole premise of the book. Neither Huck nor Mark Twain can tolerate, in imaginative terms, Jim freed. That would blast the predilection from its mooring.

Thus the fatal ending becomes the elaborate deferment of a necessary and necessarily unfree Africanist character's escape, because freedom has no meaning to Huck or to the text without the spectre of enslavement, the anodyne to individualism; the yardstick of absolute power over the life of another; the signed, marked, informing, and mutating presence of a black slave.

The novel addresses at every point in its structural edifice, and lingers over in every fissure, the slave's body and personality: the way it speaks, what passion legal or illicit it is prey to, what pain it can endure, what limits, if any, there are to its suffering, what possibilities there are for forgiveness, compassion, love. Two things strike us in this novel: the apparently limitless store of love and compassion the black man has for his white friend and white masters; and his assumption that the whites are indeed what they say they are, superior, and adult. This representation of Jim as the visible other can be read as the yearning of whites for forgiveness and love, but the yearning is made possible only when it is understood that Jim has recognized his inferiority (not as slave, but as black) and despises it. Jim permits his persecutors to torment him, humiliate him, and responds to the torment and humiliation with boundless love. The humiliation that Huck and Tom subject Jim to is baroque, endless, foolish, mind-softening – and it comes after we have experienced Jim as an adult, a caring father and a sensitive man. If Jim had been a white convict befriended by Huck, the ending could not have been imagined or written: because it would not have been possible for two children to play so painfully with the life of a white man (regardless of his class, education, or fugitiveness) once he had been revealed to us as a moral adult. Jim's slave status makes play and deferment possible – but it also dramatises, in style and mode of narration, the connection between slavery and the achievement (in actual and imaginary terms) of freedom. Jim seems unassertive, loving, irrational, passionate, dependent, inarticulate (except for the 'talks' he and Huck have, long sweet talks we are not privy to – but what did you talk about, Huck?). It is not what Jim seems that warrants inquiry, but what Mark Twain, Huck, and especially Tom need from him that should solicit our attention. In that sense the book may indeed be 'great' because in its structure, in the hell it puts its readers through at the end, the frontal debate it forces, it simulates and describes the parasitical nature of white freedom. □

Coming as it does towards the end of the twentieth century, and from a novelist of Morrison's stature, this is the most challenging reading of *Huckleberry Finn*, and especially of its ending, we are to encounter. Implicit in what Morrison is saying is the possibility that there could have been a *Huckleberry Finn* without Jim. Much of the social panorama the novel presents could have been realised if Huck had been accompanied in his adventures by Tom. Then indeed the novel could have been as open-ended as in fact it is, without any sense that it need be anything else. It is Jim who needs an end. In a novel without development or destination, Jim's plight requires both. Because of it, the drift of Twain's fatalistic comedy is intermittently brought to a self-questioning halt. To paraphrase Morrison, if Huck is really to matter, if the novel itself is really to matter, the agency for Huck's struggle must be 'the nigger Jim'. At the deepest levels of his intelligence and imagination Twain knows this, but it is Morrison's point that he cannot bring Huck through the struggle: 'neither Huck nor Mark Twain can tolerate, in imaginative terms, Jim freed.' Whether the novel eventually 'simulates and describes the parasitical nature of white freedom' may, however, be more open to question. In what sense is Huck, or even Tom, free at the end? Is it not rather the case that the novel simulates and describes the fact that if white freedom is parasitical, it will not be freedom?

CHAPTER FIVE

Huckleberry Finn: Twentieth Century Critical Response

ESLIE A. FIEDLER'S 'Come Back to the Raft Ag'in, Huck Honey!'[1] provides an appropriate transition to readings by twentieth century professional critics and academics. Its content contributes to Mailer's assertion that 'the near-burned-out, throttled, hate-filled dying affair between whites and blacks is still our great national love affair'; it is referred to explicitly by Ellison and is implicit in Morrison's comments on 'the yearning of whites for forgiveness and love'. In Fiedler's essay Cooper's *Leatherstocking Tales* and Dana's *Two Years Before the Mast* join *Moby-Dick* and *Huckleberry Finn* as books commonly found on the shelves of the children's library: 'children's books, or more precisely, boys' books'. 'What do all these books have in common?', Fiedler asks:

■ As boys books we would expect them shyly, guilelessly as it were, to proffer a chaste male love as the ultimate emotional experience – and this is spectacularly the case. In Dana, the narrator's melancholy love is the *kanaka*, Hope; in Cooper, the lifelong affection of Natty Bumppo and Chingachgook; in Melville, Ishmael's love for Queequeg; in Twain, Huck's feeling for Nigger Jim. At the focus of emotion where we are accustomed to find in the world's great novels some heterosexual passion, be it Platonic love or adultery, seduction, rape or long-drawn-out flirtation, we come instead upon the fugitive slave and the no-account boy lying side by side on a raft borne by the endless river towards an impossible escape, or the pariah sailor waking in the tattooed arms of the brown harpooner on the verge of their impossible quest. 'Aloha, Aikane, aloha nui,' Hope cries to the lover who prefers him above his fellow-whites: and Ishmael, in utter frankness, tells us: 'Thus, then, in our heart's honeymoon, lay I and Queequeg – a cosy, loving pair.' Physical it all is, certainly, yet of an ultimate innocence; there is between the lovers no sword but a childlike ignorance, as if the possibility of a fall to the carnal had not yet been discovered. Even in the *Vita Nuova* of Dante there is no vision of love less offensively, more unremittingly chaste: that it is not adult seems sometimes beside the point.

The tenderness of Huck's repeated loss and refinding of Jim, Ishmael's sensations as he wakes under the pressure of Queequeg's arm, the role of almost Edenic helpmate played for Bumppo by the Indian – these shape us from childhood: we have no sense of first discovering them, of having been once without them.

Of the infantile, the homoerotic aspects of these stories we are, though vaguely, aware, but it is only with an effort that we can wake to a consciousness of how, among us who at the level of adulthood find a difference in colour sufficient provocation for distrust and hatred they celebrate, all of them, the mutual love of *a white man and a coloured.*

So buried at a level of acceptance which does not touch reason, so desperately repressed from overt recognition, so contrary to what is usually thought of as our ultimate level of taboo – the sense of that love can survive only in the obliquity of a symbol, persistent, archetypal, in short, as a myth: the boy's homoerotic crush, the love of the black fused at this level into a single thing.

I hope I have been using here a hopelessly abused word with some precision: by myth I mean a coherent pattern of beliefs and feelings, so widely shared at a level beneath consciousness that there exists no abstract vocabulary for representing it, and (this is perhaps another aspect of the same thing) so 'sacred' that unexamined, irrational restraints inhibit any explicit analysis. Such a complex achieves a formula or pattern story, which serves both to embody it, and, at first at least, to conceal its full implications. Later the secret may be revealed, the myth (I use a single word for the formula and what is formulised) analysed or 'allegorically interpreted' according to the language of the day.

I find the situation we have been explicating genuinely mythic; certainly it has the concealed character of the true myth, eluding the wary pounce of Howells or of Mrs Twain who excised from *Huckleberry Finn* the cussin' as unfit for children, but left, unperceived, a conventionally abhorrent doctrine of ideal love. Even the writers in whom we find it, attained it, in a sense, dreaming. The felt difference between *Huckleberry Finn* and Twain's other books must lie surely in the release from conscious restraint inherent in the author's assumption of the character of Huck; the passage in and out of darkness and river mist, the constant confusion of identities (Huck's ten or twelve names – the questions of who is the real uncle, who the true Tom), the sudden intrusions into alien violences without past or future, give the whole work for all its carefully observed detail, the texture of a dream.

Ishmael and Queequeg, arm in arm, about to ship out, Huck and Jim swimming beside the raft in the peaceful flux of the Mississippi – it is the motion of water which completes the syndrome, the American dream of isolation afloat. The Negro as homoerotic lover blends with the myth of running off to sea, of running the great river down to the sea. The immensity of water defines a loneliness that demands love; its strangeness symbolises the disavowal of the conventional that makes possible all versions of love. □

At the end of this passage Fiedler is anticipating Eliot's sense of Twain's 'unconsciousness' in the writing of *Huckleberry Finn*. He makes us alive to recurrent relationships in nineteenth century American literature which, after his essay, can never be overlooked. But we need the rest of his argument:

■ In the myth, one notes finally, it is always in the role of outcast, ragged woodsman, or despised sailor (Call me Ishmael!), or unregenerate boy (Huck before the prospect of being 'sivilized' cries, 'I been here before!') that we turn to the love of a coloured man. But how, we must surely ask, does the vision of the white American as pariah correspond with our long-held public status: the world's beloved, the success? It is perhaps only the artist's portrayal of *himself,* the notoriously alienated writer in America, at home with such images, child of the town drunk, the survivor. But no. Ishmael is all of us, our unconfessed universal fear objectified in the writer's status as in the sailor's: that compelling anxiety, which every foreigner notes, that we may not be loved, that we are loved for our possessions and not ourselves, that we are really – *alone!* It is that underlying terror which explains our almost furtive incredulity in the face of adulation or favour, what is called (once more the happy adjective) our 'boyish modesty.'

Our dark-skinned beloved will take us, we assure ourselves, when we have been cut off, or have cut ourselves off from all others, without rancour or the insult of forgiveness; he will fold us in his arms saying 'Honey' or 'Aikane!', he will comfort us, as if our offense against him were long ago remitted, were never truly *real*. And yet we cannot really forget our guilt ever; the stories that embody the myth dramatise almost compulsively the role of the coloured man as victim: Dana's Hope is shown dying of the white man's syphilis; Queequeg is portrayed as racked by fever, a pointless episode except in the light of this necessity; Cooper's Indian smoulders to a hopeless old age conscious of the imminent disappearance of his race; Jim is shown loaded down with chains, weakened by the hundred torments of Tom's notion of bullyness. The immense gulf of guilt must be underlined, just as is the disparity of colour (Queequeg is not merely brown but monstrously tattooed, Chingachgook is horrid with paint, Jim is shown as the Sick Arab dyed blue), so that the final reconciliation will seem more unbelievable, more tender. The myth makes no attempt to whitewash our outrage as a fact; it portrays it as meaningless in the face of love.

There would be something insufferable, I think, in that final vision of remission if it were not for the apparent presence of a motivating anxiety, the sense always of a last chance: behind the white American's nightmare that someday, no longer tourist, inheritor, or liberator, he will be rejected, refused – he dreams of his acceptance at the breast he has most utterly offended. It is a dream so sentimental, so outrageous, so desperate that it redeems our concept of boyhood from nostalgia to tragedy,

In each generation we play out the impossible mythos, and we live to see our children play it, the white boy and the black we can discover wrestling affectionately on any American street, along which they will walk in adulthood eyes averted from each other, unwilling to touch. The dream recedes; the immaculate passion and the astonishing reconciliation become a memory, and less, a regret, at last the unrecognised motifs of a child's book. 'It's too good to be true, Honey,' Jim says to Huck, 'It's too good to be true.' □

As Wolff noted in her essay on *Tom Sawyer* it is the matriarchy that the male hero wants to escape from. He is seeking, we deduce from Fiedler, the arms of a male lover who may pass for Noble Savage. If the matriarchy can be associated with all the domestication and compromise of the Old World, the Noble Savage from the male point of view is associated with all the uncorrupted freedoms of the New. With him the white man can be as Adam before the fall, and there is no need of Eve. That such a thesis leaves women and people of colour in unacceptable positions, even though one is negative and the other apparently positive, is all too obvious. No wonder neither Ellison nor Morrison can concede to Fiedler. Along with the novelists he discusses, Fiedler comes close to imposing on the non-white the role of absolver of white guilt. What a Jim might feel about this role is hardly a question! Fiedler knows that the myth dramatises 'almost compulsively the role of the coloured man as victim'. In Morrison's words above: 'this representation of Jim as the visible other can be read as the yearning of whites for forgiveness and love, but the yearning is made possible only when it is understood that Jim has recognised his inferiority (not as slave, but as black) and despises it.' Fiedler's response to this victimisation is to insist rhapsodically that the white dream 'is a dream so sentimental, so outrageous, so desperate that it redeems our concept of boyhood from nostalgia to tragedy'. On Fiedler's terms, tragedy is the failure of an ideal love. Jim, however, might have wanted the ideal love even less than he wanted the slavery. *His* tragedy is that what he wants is not his option.

Lionel Trilling[2] takes his clue from the third of T. S. Eliot's *Four Quartets*, especially from the lines: 'I do not know much about gods; but I think that the river / Is a strong brown god . . .'

In Trilling's words,

■ Huck himself is the servant of the river-god, and he comes very close to being aware of the divine nature of the being he serves. The world he inhabits is perfectly equipped to accommodate a deity, for it is full of presences and meanings which it conveys by natural signs and also by preternatural omens and taboos: to look at the moon over the left shoulder, to shake the tablecloth after sundown, to handle a snakeskin, are ways of offending the obscure and prevalent spirits. Huck is at odds, on moral and aesthetic grounds, with the only form of Christianity he knows, and his very intense moral life may be said to derive from his love of the river. He lives in a perpetual adoration of the Mississippi's power and charm. Huck, of course, always expresses himself better than he can know, but nothing draws upon his gift of speech like his response to his deity. After every sally into the social life of the shore, he returns to the river with relief and thanksgiving; and at each return, regular and explicit as a chorus in a Greek tragedy, there is a hymn of praise to the god's beauty, mystery, and strength, and to his noble grandeur in contrast with the pettiness of men.

Generally, the god is benign: a being of long sunny days and spacious nights. But, like any god, he is also dangerous and deceptive. He generates fogs which bewilder, and he contrives echoes and false distances which confuse. His sandbars can ground and his hidden snags can mortally wound a great steamboat. He can cut away the solid earth from under a man's feet and take his house with it. The sense of the danger of the river is what saves the book from any touch of the sentimentality and moral ineptitude of most works of the imagination which contrast the life of nature with the life of society.

The river itself is only divine; it is not ethical and good. But its nature seems to foster the goodness of those who love it and try to fit themselves to its ways. And we must observe that we cannot make – that Mark Twain does not make – an absolute opposition between the river and human society, To Huck much of the charm of the river life is human: it is the raft and the wigwam and Jim. He has not run away from Miss Watson and the Widow Douglas and his brutal father to a completely individualistic liberty, for in Jim he finds his true father, very much as Stephen Dedalus in James Joyce's *Ulysses* finds his true father in Leopold Bloom.[3] The boy and the Negro slave form a family, a primitive community – and it is a community of saints. ☐

Distinguished as Trilling was, much of this might strike a reader as fanciful. Huck 'lives in a perpetual adoration of the Mississippi's power and charm'! The river's 'nature seems to foster the goodness of those who love it and try to fit themselves to its ways'! 'A community of saints'! Trilling is forcing onto the novel a source of moral certainty, deriving apparently from the river, which it does not offer. He is more accurate when he points to the danger of the river, and more profitably suggestive in seeing Jim as a father figure to Huck. This role for Jim may both qualify and supplement Fiedler's version of Jim, but it is undermined by Morrison's.

Trilling is one of the many critics who turn to the incident in the last four paragraphs of chapter 15, when Huck is rebuked by Jim for the trick Huck has tried to play after the fog:

■ This incident is the beginning of the moral testing and development which a character so morally sensitive as Huck's must inevitably undergo. And it becomes an heroic character when, on the urging of affection, Huck discards the moral code he has always taken for granted and resolves to help Jim in his escape from slavery. The intensity of his struggle over the act suggests how deeply he is involved in the society which he rejects. The satiric brilliance of the episode lies, of course, in Huck's solving his problem not by doing 'right' but by doing 'wrong.' He has only to consult his conscience, the conscience of a Southern boy in the middle of the last century, to know that he ought to return Jim to slavery. And as soon as he makes the decision according to conscience and decides to inform on Jim, he has all the warmly gratifying emotions of conscious virtue. 'Why, it was astonishing, the way I felt as light as a feather right straight off, and my troubles all gone . . . I felt good and all washed clean of sin for the first time I had ever felt so in my life, and I knew I could pray now. ☐

One's only reservation about this response is with the phrase 'satiric brilliance'. Satire is a word used frequently of *Huckleberry Finn*. Again it may suggest too much certainty on Twain's part, as if he knows where he is and is mocking those who do not. It may suggest too much authorial superiority, whereas Twain knows that multitudes of people, otherwise having the average mix of virtues and vices, have believed it was wrong to aid a fleeing slave. He has been one of these people himself and does not feel superior to them. In all of Huck's debates with himself about this issue, there is rather an authorial sense of the fundamental ironies, terrible if not funny, in which circumstances may place us.

As Trilling moves towards his conclusion, we read:

■ With the end of the Civil War capitalism had established itself. The relaxing influence of the frontier was coming to an end. Americans increasingly became 'dwellers in cities' and 'worshippers of the machine.' Mark Twain himself became a notable part of this new dispensation. No one worshipped the machine more than he did, or thought he did – he ruined himself by his devotion to the Paige type-setting machine by which he hoped to make a fortune even greater than he had made by his writing, and he sang the praises of the machine age in *A Connecticut Yankee in King Arthur's Court*. He associated intimately with the dominant figures of American business enterprise. Yet at the same time he hated the new way of life and kept bitter memoranda of his scorn, commenting on the 'low morality' or the bad taste or the smugness and dullness of the men who were shaping the national ideal and directing the destiny of the nation.

Mark Twain said of *Tom Sawyer* that it 'is simply a hymn, put into prose form to give it a worldly air.' He might have said the same, and with even more reason, of *Huckleberry Finn*, which is a hymn to an older America forever gone, an America which had its great national faults, which was full of violence and even of cruelty, but which still maintained its sense of reality, for it was not yet enthralled by money; the father of ultimate illusion and lies. Against the money-god stands the river-god whose comments are silent – sunlight, space, uncrowded time, stillness and danger. It was quickly forgotten once its practical usefulness had passed, but, as Mr Eliot's poem says, 'The river is within us . . .' □

The sentimentality of this passage suggests that, as the States begin to boom after the Second World War, it is Trilling himself who is nostalgic for an apparently simpler time. His is the kind of nostalgia Dwight MacDonald objects to in the piece on *Tom Sawyer*. Where he finds America's earlier 'sense of reality' in *Huckleberry Finn* is anyone's guess. Very obviously, the novel is full of fantasy and fraud, its very structure being as unreal as the structure of any great novel has ever been. This structure proposes that an adult runaway black slave, pressed by his own plight and that of his wife and children, would make no protest about drifting south down the Mississippi river in the company of an aimless white boy!

Indeed when Trilling addresses the structure of *Huckleberry Finn*, his defence of it, in the next passage, is formal rather than realistic. This concluding passage also discusses the novel's language:

■ In form and style *Huckleberry Finn* is an almost perfect work. Only one mistake has ever been charged against it, that it concludes with Tom Sawyer's elaborate, too elaborate, game of Jim's escape. Certainly this episode is too long – in the original draft it was much longer – and certainly it is a falling-off, as almost anything would have to be, from the incidents of the river. Yet it has a certain formal aptness – like, say, that of the Turkish initiation which brings Molière's *Le Bourgeois Gentilhomme* to its close. It is a rather mechanical development of an idea, and yet some device is needed to permit Huck to return to his anonymity, to give up the role of hero, to fall into the background which he prefers, for he is modest in all things and could not well endure the attention and glamour which attend a hero at a book's end. For this purpose nothing could serve better than the mind of Tom Sawyer with its literary furnishings, its conscious romantic desire for experience and the hero's part, and its ingenious schematisation of life to achieve that aim.

The form of the book is based on the simplest of all novel-forms, the so-called picaresque novel, or novel of the road, which strings its incidents on the line of the hero's travels. But, as Pascal says, 'rivers are roads that move, and the movement of the road in its own mysterious life transmutes the primitive simplicity' of the form: the road itself is the greatest character in this novel of the road, and the hero's departures from the river and his returns to it compose a subtle and significant pattern. The linear simplicity of the picaresque novel is further modified by the story's having a clear dramatic organisation: it has a beginning, a middle and an end, and a mounting suspense of interest.

As for the style of the book, it is not less than definitive in American literature. The prose of *Huckleberry Finn* established for written prose the virtues of American colloquial speech. This has nothing to do with pronunciation or grammar. It has something to do with ease and freedom in the use of language. Most of all it has to do with the structure of the sentence, which is simple, direct, and fluent, maintaining the rhythm of the word-groups of speech and the intonations of the speaking voice.

In the matter of language, American literature had a special problem. The young nation was inclined to think that the mark of the truly literary product was a grandiosity and elegance not to be found in the common speech. It therefore encouraged a greater breach between its vernacular and its literary language than, say, English literature of the same period ever allowed. This accounts for the hollow ring one now and then hears even in the work of our best writers in the first half of the last century. English writers of equal stature would never have made the lapses into rhetorical excess that are common in Cooper and Poe and that are to be found even in Melville and Hawthorne.

Yet at the same time that the language of ambitious literature was high and thus always in danger of falseness, the American reader was keenly interested in the actualities of daily speech. No literature, indeed, was ever so taken up with matters of speech as ours was. 'Dialect,' which attracted even our serious writers, was the accepted common ground of our popular humorous writing. Nothing in social life seemed so remarkable as the different forms which speech could take – the brogue of the immigrant Irish or the mispronunciation of the German, the 'affectation' of the English, the reputed precision of the Bostonian, the legendary twang of the Yankee farmer, and the drawl of the 'Pike County' man. Mark Twain, of course, was in the tradition of humour that exploited this interest, and no-one could play with it nearly so well. Although today the carefully spelled-out dialects of nineteenth-century American humour are likely to seem dull enough, the subtle variations of speech of *Huckleberry Finn*, of which Mark Twain was justly proud, are still part of the liveliness and flavour of the book.

Out of his knowledge of the actual speech of America Mark Twain forged a classic prose. The adjective may seem a strange one, yet it is apt. Forget the misspellings and the faults of grammar, and the prose will be seen to move with the greatest simplicity, directness, lucidity and grace. These qualities are by no means accidental, Mark Twain, who read widely, was passionately interested in the problems of style; the mark of the strictest literary sensibility is everywhere to be found in the prose of *Huckleberry Finn*. □

Trilling's last paragraph, not quoted here, refers to the famous Hemingway pronouncement and goes on to justify it. He has already made his most important point when, in the above passage, he speaks of the 'breach' between America's 'vernacular and its literary language'. This breach is another aspect of the problem of artistic form in nineteenth century American literature. If its forms, like its language, tended towards the artificial or the unreal, it was because they had to be invented. Unlike English literature, American literature inherited no patterns which had been so validated by history as to seem authoritative. What had been inherited had its authoritative source elsewhere. So in *Huckleberry Finn* we have the immediacies captured by the vernacular. What structure of things these immediacies belong to remains an irresolvable question.

Like Eliot a couple of years later, Trilling offers a formal defence of the ending of *Huckleberry Finn*. Both are condemned for this by Leo Marx.[4] Marx believes that 'the ending of *Huckleberry Finn* makes so many readers uneasy because they rightly sense that it jeopardises the significance of the entire novel':

■ The meaning is not in the least obscure, it is made explicit again and again. The very words with which Clemens launches Huck and Jim upon their voyage indicate that theirs is not a boy's lark but a quest for freedom. From the electrifying moment when Huck comes back to Jackson's Island and rouses Jim with the news that a search party is on the way, we are meant to believe that Huck is enlisted in the cause of freedom. 'Git up and hump yourself, Jim!' he cries, 'There ain't a minute to lose, They're after us!' What particularly counts here is the *us*. No one is after Huck: no one but Jim knows he is alive. In that small word Clemens compresses the exhilarating power of Huck's instinctive humanity. His unpremeditated identification with Jim's flight from slavery is an unforgettable moment in American experience, and it may be said at once that any culmination of the journey which detracts from the urgency and dignity with which it begins will necessarily be unsatisfactory.

The most obvious thing wrong with the ending, then, is the flimsy contrivance by which Clemens frees Jim. In the end we not only discover that Jim has been a free man for two months, but that his freedom has been granted by old Miss Watson. If this were only a mechanical device for terminating the action, it might not call for much comment. But it is more than that: it is a significant clue to the import of the last ten chapters. Remember who Miss Watson is. She is the Widow's sister whom Huck introduces in the first pages of the novel. It is she who keeps 'pecking' at Huck, who tries to teach him to spell and to pray and to keep his feet off the furniture. She is an ardent proselytiser for piety and good manners, and her greed provides the occasion for the journey in the first place. She is Jim's owner, and he decides to flee only when he realises that she is about to break her word (she cannot resist a slave trader's offer of eight hundred dollars) and sell him down the river away from his family.

Miss Watson in short, is the Enemy. If we except a predilection for physical violence, she exhibits all the outstanding traits of the valley society. She pronounces the polite lies of civilisation that suffocate Huck's spirit. The freedom which Jim seeks, and which Huck and Jim temporarily enjoy aboard the raft, is accordingly freedom *from* everything for which Miss Watson stands. Indeed, the very intensity of the novel derives from the discordance between the aspirations of the fugitives and the respectable code for which she is a spokesman. Therefore, her regeneration, of which the deathbed freeing of Jim is the unconvincing sign, hints a resolution of the novel's essential conflict. Perhaps because this device most transparently reveals that shift in point of view which he could not avoid, and which is less easily discerned elsewhere in the concluding chapters, Clemens plays it down. He makes little attempt to account for Miss Watson's change of heart, a change particularly surprising in view of Jim's brazen escape. Had Clemens given this episode dramatic emphasis appropriate to its function, Miss Watson's bestowal of freedom upon Jim would have proclaimed what the rest of the ending actually accomplishes – a vindication of persons and attitudes Huck and Jim had symbolically repudiated when they set forth downstream. □

'Theirs is not a boy's lark but a quest for freedom'. Marx's is a wilfully realistic reading of the novel. Immediately following 'They're after us' at the very end of chapter 11, we have chapters 12, 13 and 14 dealing with the adventures aboard the *Walter Scott* and Huck's arguments with Jim about kings and dukes and King Solomon. None of this is the stuff of a realistic quest for freedom. No actual escaped slave would get himself involved in these *Tom Sawyer* adventures and routines. Even if Marx did not know that Twain had written this material at the end and inserted it towards the beginning, he might have seen that, positioned where it is, it already disrupts his kind of reading long before he gets to the ending. Indeed Marx's reading is also disrupted once Huck and Jim go past Cairo and continue southwards, a direction in which Jim has no hope of freedom. In *Huckleberry Finn* Twain is not confined to the realistic, whatever that would be. As well as a quest for freedom he is doing other things. In a New World, the meaning of which is all to be imagined, and in which huge territorial areas have already scripted a reality requiring slavery, he is probing the limits of language and creativity. What is the restraint on these forces in emerging territory, where a sense of governing order is always disputable? In such territory who can separate the real from the imagined, the true from the false? Is it only predilection, and nothing absolute, which enables a reader like Marx to decide that in *Huckleberry Finn* some words are better than others? Twain's novel, if unconsciously so, is as radical as Joyce's *Ulysses*, because it forces these issues. Ironically, when it offers a conventional reality, Miss Watson undergoing an exemplary change of heart, Marx objects, as if anything else but such changes of heart on a mass scale will do away with slavery and racism. Huck and Jim's personal quest, compelling as it sometimes is, is an insignificant pulse in this needed transformation. It is to be taken seriously, but not too seriously. Its eventual forlornness is shared by Miss Watson's deathbed conversion. Think what she could have achieved in life. But ponder also the validity of belief itself, when the eradication of slavery and racism is dependent on people believing the opposite of what they once believed, and with equal conviction.

Marx continues:

■ On the raft the escaped slave and the white boy try to practice their code; 'What you want, above all things, on a raft, is for everybody to be satisfied and feel right and kind towards the others.' This human credo constitutes the paramount affirmation of *The Adventures of Huckleberry Finn*, and it obliquely aims a devastating criticism at the existing social order. It is a creed which Huck and Jim bring to the river. It neither emanates from nature nor is it addressed to nature. Therefore I do not see that it means much to talk about the river as a god in this novel. The river's connection with this high aspiration for man is that it provides a means of escape, a place where the code can be tested. The truly profound meanings of the novel are generated by the impingement of the actual world of slavery: feuds, lynching, murder, and a spurious Christian morality upon the ideal of the raft. The result is a tension which somehow demands release in the novel's ending.

But Clemens was unable to effect this release and at the same time control the central theme. The unhappy truth about the ending of *Huckleberry Finn*, is that the author, having revealed the tawdry nature of the culture of the great valley, yielded to its essential complacency. The general tenor of the closing scenes, to which the token regeneration of Miss Watson is merely one superficial clue, amounts to just that. In fact, this entire reading of *Huckleberry Finn* merely confirms the brilliant insight of George Santayana, who many years ago spoke of American humorists, of whom he considered Mark Twain an outstanding representative, as having only 'half escaped' the genteel tradition. Santayana meant that men like Clemens were able to 'point to what contradicts it in the facts; but not in order to abandon the genteel tradition, for they have nothing solid to put in its place.' This seems to me the real key to the failure of *Huckleberry Finn*. Clemens had presented the contrast between the two social orders but could not, or would not, accept the tragic fact that the one he had rejected was an image of solid reality and the other an ecstatic dream. Instead, he gives us the cosy reunion with Aunt Polly in a scene fairly bursting with approbation of the entire family, the Phelpses included. Like Miss Watson, the Phelpses are almost perfect specimens of the dominant culture. They are kind to their friends and relatives; they have no taste for violence; they are people capable of devoting themselves to their spectacular dinners while they keep Jim locked in the little hut down by the ash hopper with its lone window boarded up. (Of course Aunt Sally visits Jim to see if he is 'comfortable,' and Uncle Silas comes in 'to pray with him.') These people, with their comfortable Sunday-dinner conviviality and the runaway slave padlocked nearby, are reminiscent of those solid German citizens we have heard about in our time who tried to maintain a similarly *gemütlich* way of life within virtual earshot of Buchenwald. I do not mean to imply that Clemens was unaware of the shabby morality of such people. After the abortive escape of Jim, when Tom asks about him, Aunt Sally replies: 'Him? . . .

the runaway nigger? . . . They've got him back, safe and sound, and he's in the cabin again, on bread and water, and loaded down with chains, till he's claimed or sold!' Clemens understood people like the Phelpses, but nevertheless he was forced to rely upon them to provide his happy ending. The satisfactory outcome of Jim's quest for freedom must be attributed to the benevolence of the very people whose inhumanity first made it necessary. □

It is refreshing to have the 'talk about the river as a god' knocked on the head. Even so, Marx does want to simplify. His identification of Miss Watson as 'the Enemy' in the previous quotation is continued here with his denunciation of riverbank society. Whether genteel or not, this society for Twain is representative. Essentially, it is what human beings gathered together are like; no better, no worse. Maybe Marx, 'within virtual earshot of Buchenwald', would have been of the best. It is a matter of how superior to a given set of people one can feel one is, or would be. *Huckleberry Finn* has one character, Colonel Sherburn, who really feels himself superior, and his murderous authoritarianism in chapters 21 and 22 takes no prisoners. Huck by contrast hardly ever feels superior. He just wants to get away, though there may be nowhere else to be. Who, after all, can settle for a drifting raft?

In his essay ('Remarks on the Sad Initiation of Huckleberry Finn') James M. Cox develops in *Huckleberry Finn* the thesis about *Tom Sawyer* already referred to. Again he releases Twain from a realistic straitjacket, reading the later novel in terms of its repetition and variation of central themes. Commenting on Huck's faking of his own death to escape his father, Cox writes:

■ This fake murder is probably the most vital and crucial incident of the entire novel. Having killed himself, Huck is 'dead' throughout the entire journey down the river. He is indeed the man without identity who is reborn at almost every river bend, not because he desires a new role, but because he must re-create himself to elude the forces which close in on him from every side. The rebirth theme becomes the driving idea behind the entire action.

Coupled with and inseparable from the theme of rebirth is the central image of death. Huck has hardly assumed the role of outcast when he meets Jim, who is also in frantic flight (interestingly enough, Jim is considered in terms of property too; his motive for escaping was fear of being sold down the river for $800.00), and the two fugitives watch the house of death float by on the swollen Mississippi. When Jim carefully covers up the face of the dead man in the house, the second major image of the novel is forged. These two images, rebirth and death, provide a frame for all succeeding episodes of the arduous initiation. As Huck and Jim move down the river an oncoming steamboat crashes into their raft, forcing the two outcasts to swim for their lives. From this baptism Huck emerges to enter the new life at the Grangerfords under the name of George Jackson. His final act in that life is to cover the dead face of Buick Grangerford much as Jim had covered Pap's face in the house of death. When the Duke and King come aboard, their unscrupulous schemes force Huck and Jim to appear in new disguises; but the image of death is never absent. It confronts Huck in the little 'one-horse town' in Arkansas where Colonel Sherburn shoots the drunken Boggs in cold blood. When the townspeople lift Boggs from the street and take him to the little drug store, Huck peers in through the window to watch him die. The Peter Wilks episode involves the same central images. The Duke and the King disguise themselves as foreign kinsmen of the deceased Wilks and they force Huck to play the role of an English valet. The final scene of the episode takes place in the graveyard where the mob of townsmen has gathered to exhume the buried Wilks in an effort to discover whether the Duke and King are impostors. A flash of lightning reveals the dead man with the gold on his breast where Huck had hidden it. The man who has Huck in charge forgets his prisoner in his zeal to see corpse and gold; Huck takes full advantage of the moment and runs out of that world forever.

Finally, at the Phelps farm the initiation is completed. Huck is reborn as Tom Sawyer and this time no image of death appears. The Duke and the King are far back in his past and the wheel has indeed come full circle. Jim is imprisoned in a cabin much like the one in which Pap locked Huck; Tom Sawyer himself comes to the rescue in the role of Sid Sawyer: the entire household, though not the same as the one in which the novel began, is related to it through strong blood ties. The full import of this initiation becomes more clearly evident when the differences between Huck and Tom Sawyer are examined. □

As Cox sees it,

■ Huck is, in the deepest sense, an outcast. Although Tom is an orphan he at least has relatives who recognise his credentials and have adopted him.

Huck has only Pap, the drunkard, the outcast himself, whose eyes shine through his tangled, greasy hair 'like he was behind vines.' Pap attains intense symbolic stature in his brief but violent pilgrimage:

> . . . There warn't no color in his face. Where his face showed: it was white; not like another man's white, but a white to make a body's

flesh crawl – a tree toad white, a fishbelly white. As for his clothes – just rags, that was all.

There is in this description a supernatural quality which links Pap to Melville's whale. His ways are not so much evil as they are inscrutable; he has somehow gotten consumed by the very nature he set out to conquer, and out of the dark union between himself and the River the divine Huck has sprung; Huck certainly belongs more to the river than to the society along its banks, but this in no way makes of him a Rousseauistic child of nature. His lineal descendancy from Pap removes him from the garden of innocence, but if it implies his connection with violence and terror, it also puts him in touch with the deeper human forces which cannot be neatly filed under sociological headings. He has 'connections' which, though they do not enable him to get ahead in an acquisitive society, give him a depth and a reality which far surpass anything Tom Sawyer has dreamed of. □

The link with Melville's whale has to overcome too much incongruity, but Cox is right to insist on the inscrutability of Pap and thereby resist the too simple moral condemnation to which critics generally subject this character. Pap's self-consciousness in chapter 6 suggests that his frenzied states are partially self-induced, even to the point of fearful hallucination. Perhaps his most exciting life is with the demons which then possess him, taking him into depths of dread in which he chases Huck round and round the cabin 'calling me the Angel of Death'. It is true, in Cox's words, that 'no Rousseauistic child of nature' could be Pap's offspring, yet what does Cox mean by 'the divine Huck'? It seems impossible to give meaning to the adjective.

Developing the differences between Huck and Tom, Cox asserts:

■ There is bitter irony in Huck's assumption of Tom's name because the values of Tom Sawyer are so antithetical to the values of Huck Finn; in the final analysis, the two boys cannot exist in the same world. When Huck regains his own identity at the very end of the novel he immediately feels the compulsion to 'light out for the territory' because he knows that to be Huck Finn is to be the outcast beyond the paling fences. From Mark Twain's point of view in this novel, Tom Sawyer's civilisation involves obedience, imitation, and is directly opposed to a dynamic and creative frontier imagination. In Tom Sawyer's triumph the hard core of Mark Twain's later disillusion and pessimism is already evident. Although Huck Finn may escape to the territory, the whole outline of the frontier is receding westward before the surge of a small town culture, and it is indeed doomed country into which Huck must retreat.

Huck Finn cannot be reduced to historical proportions, however, even though there is much in the novel for the historian. The territory to which Huck refers is more than a diminishing area in nineteenth century America. It is a metaphorical equivalent of the broader and deeper vision which Huck and Jim represent. To be in the 'territory' is not to be in heaven, for the wilderness and waste places have their perils for the sojourner, as Pap's presence fearfully testifies, but it is to escape the dehumanising forces of the little towns, it is to be stripped of the pride encouraged by a sterile respectability and to feel absolute humility in the face of the awful unseen powers. Huck and Jim are the only real human beings in the novel – they are human because they can still feel and because they possess a heightened sensitivity to the promises and terrors of life. The characters whom they encounter, with the exception of the young and innocent, have an angularity and rigidity which mark them as grotesques. The blind spots of the eminently respectable become proving grounds for the avaricious; the pretentious righteousness of one group merely encourages the brutal sensationalism of another. Only Huck and Jim possess wholeness of spirit among the horde of fragmentary personalities which parade through the novel. The society which hotly pursues Huck and Jim knows that they possess the real secrets – that is why it so desperately wants to 'own' them.

And if Tom has taken Sid's role and Huck has been forced to take Tom's in this rather discouraging progression, who is left to take Huck's place? Fifteen years later Mark Twain could not answer the question, for his imagination had been consumed by what Bernard DeVoto calls the symbols of despair. There is someone, however, to take Huck's place in this novel; he is, of course, that primitive of primitives: Jim. He stands in relation to Huck in this novel much as Huck stood in relation to Tom in *Tom Sawyer*, and is in many ways the central figure in the book. It is to Jim that Huck retreats as if to a saviour; he it is who mothers Huck as they travel down the big river: and he it is who, knowing secretly that Huck's Pap is dead forever, takes Huck to his own bosom to nourish him through the ordeal of being lost. Acting as Huck's foster father, Jim brings to that role a warmth and gentleness which Huck had never known under the brutal masculinity of his real father. Near the end of the novel, after Jim has accompanied and protected Huck on their perilous journey, how appropriate it is that he should be led back to the Phelps plantation, following his temporary escape with Tom, arrayed in the dress which the boys had stolen from Aunt Sally. The incident points to the ambivalent nature of Jim, emphasising his role of motherly father to Huck. Leslie Fiedler, looking at the novel as an American myth of love has searchingly explored this ambivalent relationship.

Jim is also one of the two great human forces in the book. By means of his truth and sincerity, the fraud and hoax of the world along the river banks are thrown into sharp relief. Probably the finest example of Jim's function as a moral norm occurs on the raft just before the King and Duke meet the country boy who unwittingly directs them into the Peter Wilks exploit. Huck awakens at daybreak one morning to see Jim grieving to himself. Jim finally tells him that a whacking sound he heard on shore reminded him of the time he disciplined his little daughter for not obeying a command. Upon repeating his command to no avail Jim finally struck the child down, only to find that her recent attack of scarlet fever had left her deaf and dumb:

> Oh, Huck, I burst out a-crying en grab her up in my arms, en say, 'Oh, de po' little thing! De Lord God Almighty forgive po' ole Jim, kaze he never gwyne to fogive hisself as long's he live!' Oh, she was plumb deef en dumb, Huck, plumb deef en dumb – en I'd ben-a-treat'n her so!

Immediately after this burst of genuine remorse, the Duke and the King launch their expedition to rob the Wilks daughters of their inheritance by pretending to be Peter Wilks's foreign kinsmen. The Duke poses as a deaf mute. By employing the same device he used so successfully in *Tom Sawyer*, Twain establishes a subtle and exquisite relationship between the two episodes. Through Jim's sensitivity the entire Wilks episode is thrown into much more precise focus. Indeed, Jim is the conscience of the novel, the spiritual yardstick by which all men are measured. As the two fugitives move down the river, Huck's whole moral sense grows out of and revolves around the presence of Jim, and his ability to measure up signifies his worth. Huck's whole sense of wrong, his feeling of guilt are products of his intimate association with Jim – his companionship with the runaway slave makes possible his moral growth.

Many critics, intent on seeing Jim as a symbol of the tragic consequences of slavery, have failed to see that he is much more than this. He is that great residue of primitive, fertile force turned free at the end of the novel at the very moment Huck is captured. That Mark Twain recognized in the novel a new American protagonist is evident not only in his creation of Jim, but in his interesting return to the whole problem of slavery in *Pudd'nhead Wilson*. Certainly Jim and Thomas à Becket Driscoll stand solidly behind Faulkner, Robert Penn Warren, and Richard Wright. Having been thrown from his secure place within the social structure, Jim will be the new fugitive which the bourgeoisie will, with a great deal of hesitation, wish to make respectable. □

Twain's later disillusionment and pessimism develop from Tom's triumph, because that triumph is always going to be a sham, a convention, substituting frenzied role play for real vitality. At the same time Huck's initiation is 'sad' (Cox's title), because the territory where he finds a vital life is losing out to Tom Sawyer. Having acknowledged history, however, Cox, with impressive eloquence, makes the essential argument for a metaphorical reading of the novel in which Huck and Jim are the only real human beings in it. In this argument Jim is the character in whom all human divisions, including those between mother and father, are healed. Cox is supplementing Fiedler's reading of the novel 'as an American myth of love'. Like Fiedler, and like Ellison in one of his readings, he believes Jim is much more than 'a symbol of the tragic consequences of slavery, . . . He is that great residue of primitive, fertile force turned free at the end of the novel at the very moment Huck is captured.' This conclusion is a reversal of what Morrison is to say, and, since it is impossible at the end to see Jim as Cox sees him, Morrison is the more persuasive. Cox, none the less, makes a provocative connection, when he sees a black man, Jim, as the 'new fugitive', replacing the forlorn, white Huck, and presumably looking forward to Wright's character, Bigger Thomas, in *Native Son*.

Cox concludes by turning to the problem of the ending of the novel:

■ The flatness of the ending results from Tom's domination of the action and the style. As soon as he appears, his whole aggressive spirit bids for position, and although Mark Twain attempts to use Huck to exploit the ironies of the situation, Tom's seizure of the style damages the tenor of the novel. It is a stylistic rather than a structural flaw, a failure in taste rather than in conception. Mark Twain's failure in taste at this particular juncture bears further consideration. *Huckleberry Finn* is without question his greatest work, and diametric opposition of Tom and Huck is eminently clear. The substitution of Tom's humour for Huck's vision indicates that Mark Twain, though aware of the two sets of values, could not keep a proper balance between them because of his fascination with Tom Sawyer. In turning over the narration to Huck Finn he had turned to the incorruptible part of himself which was not for sale and could not be bought. The opening paragraph of the novel indicates that he was not entirely unaware of what he was about:

You don't know about me without you have read a book by the name of *The Adventures of Tom Sawyer* but that ain't no matter. That book was made by Mr Mark Twain, and he told the truth, mainly. There was things which he stretched, but mainly he told the truth.

'Mainly he told the truth.' In his novel Mark Twain tried to tell the whole truth through Huckleberry Finn. Although Tom Sawyer makes his presence too much felt at the end of the novel, Mark Twain saw his whole truth with supreme vision. Because of the deeply human values which are at stake, neither the satire nor the humour is tainted by the scoffing disillusion and the adolescent cynicism in which he finally foundered. The unobtrusive formal perfection allows the novel to retain the primitive power and immediacy of the myth which it recreates: its impact strikes us in the profoundest areas of our consciousness, and we are reminded of the darkness and the terror and the violence which stalk the virgin forest where the American dream lies waiting, aware and unaware.[5] □

'Failure in taste' on the one hand; 'unobtrusive formal perfection' on the other. These are unusual bedfellows in the same novel. Presumably the Wilks episode, which Cox earlier claimed to be thrown into precise focus by Jim's sensitivity, was also a failure in taste, for Twain seems to enjoy it as much as he enjoys the ending of the novel. It does not seem that he is remembering Jim's deaf and dumb child as he writes it. How could Huckleberry Finn be the incorruptible part of Twain, when that very part is persistently corrupted by Tom Sawyer? *Huckleberry Finn* is unlike any other novel in that it hardly allows us even to infer its terms of existence. We can never be sure how it is asking to be read. Like Cox, one of Twain's very best readers, we may find ourselves inevitably imposing terms on it.

In what has been a very influential reading, Henry Nash Smith[6] engages with the novel's form in a different way from Cox. Narrative form is Smith's immediate subject. It is a development of Leo Marx, but altogether more complicated:

■ The implied denunciation of slavery in *Huckleberry Finn* is more damaging than the frontal attack delivered by *Uncle Tom's Cabin* because Jim is so much more convincing as a character than is Mrs. Stowe's Uncle Tom, who is almost an allegorical figure – a Black Christ. Yet if we read *Huckleberry Finn* simply as the story of Huck's and Jim's quest for freedom we run into difficulties. For in the last section (Chapters XXXIII–XLIII) Mark Twain seems to be burlesquing his own plot. Huck's efforts to help Jim escape, involving real danger and anguished inner conflict with the boy's conscience, give way to the elaborate foolishness of Tom Sawyer's schemes for conducting an Evasion according to rules he has deduced from *The Count of Monte Cristo* and other melodramatic works of fiction. Jim is reduced to the status of a 'darkey' in a minstrel show; the reader is evidently expected to laugh at his discomforts from the rats and spiders Tom introduces as stage properties. And at the last moment it is revealed that Jim was freed two months before through the highly implausible deathbed repentance of his owner, Miss Watson. We feel as badly sold as did the audience for the Duke's and the King's presentation of *The Royal Nonesuch*. □

So influential has Smith's reading been, the term 'Evasion' has become common currency in accounts of *Huckleberry Finn*'s final chapters. What now follows from Smith is an implicit challenge to Marx:

■ Indeed, Jim's quest for freedom receives such cavalier treatment in the Phelps plantation sequence that one is forced to ask whether it is the true imaginative centre of the story. If we examine the place which the theme of Jim's escape occupies in the book as a whole, we discover that it is by no means always central to the action. The first seven chapters, where the author has to manage the transition from the state of affairs at the end of *Tom Sawyer* to the quite different atmosphere of the sequel, offered no occasion for dealing with the new problem. Not until Huck makes his Robinson Crusoe-like discovery of Jim's campfire in Chapter VIII does the reader know that Jim has run away. We then have eight chapters during which the two friends make their way southward on the raft, with pauses for such episodes as the exploration of the 'House of Death' and the wrecked steamboat *Walter Scott*. But at the end of Chapter XVI Mark Twain faced a crisis in the management of his plot, for at this point he must have discovered that the original plan of his narrative would no longer serve his purposes.

Early in Chapter XVI Huck and Jim are approaching the mouth of the Ohio at Cairo, Illinois. Jim is understandably excited. He has conceived the idea that 'he'd be a free man the minute he seen it [Cairo], but if he missed it he'd be in the slave country again and no more show for freedom'.[7] Jim's notion that he would be free as soon as he entered the mouth of the Ohio was oversimplified, but that river was certainly his pathway to freedom. It made no sense for Huck and Jim to move a single mile farther past the mouth of the Ohio than they were forced to. If Mark Twain took Jim down the Mississippi he committed himself to a narrative plan that was very unlikely to lead Jim to freedom. His only alternatives would be to leave Jim in slavery (which, however faithful to historical probability, would have created a sombre ending quite out of keeping with the comic tone of the book), or to free him by some such *deus ex machina* device as the supposed deathbed repentance of Miss Watson.

Why then did Mark Twain not cause Huck and Jim to make their way up the Ohio? To ask this question is to answer it: he did not know the Ohio. But he had known the lower Mississippi intimately for four years as cub and pilot. As Huck and Jim float past Cairo, Mark Twain's desire to write a story drawing upon his memories of the lower Mississippi comes into conflict with the idea of telling the story of Jim's escape from slavery. When he wrote Chapter XVI he apparently did not see any escape from the dilemma. 'By-and-by' says Huck, 'we talked about what we better do, and found there warn't no way but just to go along down with the raft till we got a chance to buy a canoe to go back in.'

This plan represents a dead end for the original plan of escape. The destruction of the raft at the end of Chapter XVI registers the author's recognition of the fact. □

Smith's quantifying of the chapters in which Jim's quest for freedom is the centre of interest should cause us to check the accuracy of our engagement with the novel. It is true that what remains in the imagination may not be measurable in numbers of pages, but at last in Smith we have a reader who is aware that after chapter 16 the plot to get Jim into the free States is aborted. Smith has read Blair and knows Twain abandoned the novel at chapter 16.

What follows became perhaps the most renowned explanation of the later chapters of *Huckleberry Finn*:

■ But the journey which begins in Chapter XIX is quite different from the journey described in Chapters XII–XVI, for it has nothing to do with Jim's escape and therefore no purpose in the sense that the journey from St. Petersburg to Cairo had a purpose. Once Mark Twain had worked out in his mind a plausible device for taking Huck and Jim downstream, he seems to have forgotten about the original plan of escape up the Ohio. Even before the Duke and the King enter the story, when Huck and Jim set out on the raft from the Grangerford plantation, the earlier plan has sunk from sight. Huck now says that as soon as the raft had got out to the middle of the River, 'we . . . judged that we was free and safe once more. . . . We said there warn't no home like a raft, after all. Other places do seem so cramped up and smothery, but a raft don't. You feel mighty free and easy and comfortable on a raft.' When Huck goes ashore in Chapter XIX to look for berries, just before he meets the Duke and the King, he mentions finding a canoe without giving any indication that this is precisely what he and Jim need to make their way upstream. It should be emphasised that these incidents occur before Mark Twain has actually brought into play his device of subjecting Huck and Jim to the coercion of the Duke and the King. Thereafter, although theoretically Huck and Jim might be expected to seize the first opportunity of escaping from their captors in order to head back upstream, we are not surprised that they fail to do so. When they momentarily elude the Duke and the King after the Wilks episode (at the end of Chapter XXIX), Huck says: '. . . away we went, a sliding down the river, and it *did* seem so good to be free again and all by ourselves on the big river and nobody to bother us.'

In these moments of spontaneous reflection Huck has simply forgotten Jim's assertion that below Cairo 'he'd be in the slave country again and no more show for freedom.' What has happened is that Mark Twain has abandoned his original narrative plan and has substituted for it a different structural principle. During the journey from the Grangerford plantation to Pikesville, the action is not dictated by the reasonable if risky plan for Jim's escape but by the powerful image of Huck and Jim's 'a sliding down the river,' 'free and easy' on the raft. This image now embodies the only meaning which freedom and safety have in the narrative. It becomes the positive value replacing the original goal of actual freedom for Jim. The new goal is a subjective state, having its empirical basis in the solitude of the friends in their 'home' on 'the big river' but consisting in a mode of experience rather than an outward condition. There is some suggestion, to be sure, of a pastoral sanction for the state of mind attained by Huck and Jim when they are alone on the raft, The physical setting, the River, sometimes becomes vaguely but powerfully benign, as in the ecstatic opening of Chapter XIX. But the journey, considered as movement from one determinate place to another, has lost its meaning. It literally leads nowhere. The Phelps plantation where it ends, from the standpoint of geography eleven hundred miles downstream from St. Petersburg, is from the standpoint of Mark Twain's imagination very near the starting-point of Huck's and Jim's journey. It is his fictional rendering of the farm of his Uncle John Quarles, thirty miles inland from Hannibal, where he spent summers as a child.

The new structural principle which supplants the original linear movement toward freedom is bipolar. It is a contrast between the raft – connoting freedom, security, happiness, and harmony with physical nature – and the society of the towns along the shore, connoting vulgarity and malice and fraud and greed and violence. The raft, when those invaders from the shore, the Duke and King, can be got out of the way or even just put to sleep, is always the same. The towns are very much alike also; Pokeville, Bricksville, and Peter Wilks's home town, all embody Mark Twain's memories of Hannibal. Huck is drawn ashore repeatedly, and repeatedly returns to the raft, but this apparent movement is merely an oscillation between two modes of experience, and the successive episodes are restatements, with variations, of the same theme: the raft versus the town, the River versus the Shore. Yet this thematic plan is not so different as it might seem at first glance from the original narrative plan of linear movement toward a geographical goal. The book has a basic unity of theme despite Mark Twain's pronounced shift in overt structure. For not only does the River connote freedom; the Shore connotes slavery, bondage in a more general sense than the actual servitude of Jim. Huck and Jim share a common quest, not merely because Huck is helping Jim, but because Huck too is fleeing from slavery. On occasion it is implied that the contrast between freedom and slavery is even more general, that Jim's and Huck's predicament is that of every man, and their quest a universal human undertaking. □

As Smith sees it, *Huckleberry Finn* is not after all a journey narrative, for the raft is going nowhere. All the towns on the shore are variations of the same town: 'the new structural principle which supplants the original movement towards freedom is bipolar'; the river is freedom, the shore slavery 'in a more general sense than the actual servitude of Jim'. His point about the journey's lack of purpose and movement is confirmed by the absence of topographical change, or indeed of topography at all, with the notable exception of the first paragraph of chapter 31. Even so, it is not true that Huck's flight from slavery is equivalent to, or inclusive of, Jim's. Whatever metaphoric licence is exploited, to be a slave to society is not to be a chattel slave. Nor is it convincing to speak of Huck and Jim as subject 'to the coercion of the Duke and the King'. Realistically, it would not have been impossible for the resourceful Huck to have given these two the slip. Because of his view of life on the shore as slavery, Smith's reading proceeds towards a very moralistic response to all the people who live on the banks of the river. It has no time for the fun of much of what goes on. Even to live on the shore seems heinous. He is more persuasive, however, when he extends the bipolarity to Huck himself:

■ With respect to the great issue of the overt action, Jim's escape from slavery, Huck is divided against himself. His inner freedom is menaced by attitudes imposed upon him by society. The culture of the Shore had invaded his personality by implanting in him a conscience which is the internalised mores of the community. When Huck faces a crisis of decision about his loyalty to Jim, his conscience significantly addresses him in the language of the official culture, a tawdry and faded effort at a high style that is the rhetorical equivalent of the ornaments of the Grangerford parlour. The following sentence, for example (in Chapter XXXI), has a complexity of structure which is foreign to Huck's own mode of speech, as are the cant theological phrases:

'And at last, when it hit me all of a sudden that here was the plain hand of Providence slapping me in the face and letting me know my wickedness was being watched all the time from up there in heaven, whilst I was stealing a poor old woman's nigger that hadn't ever done me no harm, and now was showing me there's One that's always on the lookout and ain't agoing to allow no such miserable doings to go only just so fur and no further, I most dropped in my tracks I was so scared.'

Parallel clauses are built up to a monitory climax in a pattern Huck must have heard used by preachers and politicians:

'It was because my heart warn't right; it was because I warn't square; it was because I was playing double. I was letting on to give up sin, but away inside of me I was holding on to the biggest one of all. I was trying to make my mouth say I would do the right thing and the clean thing, and go and write to that nigger's owner and tell where he was; but deep down in me I knowed it was a lie – and He knowed it. You can't pray a lie – I found that out.'

In passages such as these, the polar opposition between the River and the Shore, between freedom and bondage, is restated as a division within Huck's own mind. The intuitive self, the spontaneous impulse from the deepest levels of the personality, is placed in opposition to the acquired conscience, the overlayer of prejudice and false valuation imposed upon all members of society in the name of religion, morality, law, and culture. Huck's triumph over his conscience is his most nearly heroic moment, falling short of grandeur only because his youth and ignorance prevent him from undertaking a decisive action.

What is the source of the power by which the true self triumphs over the false conscience? It is conveyed indirectly a few lines later, in a passage which is the emotional and thematic climax of the book, and one of its supremely beautiful moments. This is the voice of freedom, spontaneity, autonomy of the individual; of brotherhood, of the River as opposed to the Shore. Huck actually writes a letter to Miss Watson giving Jim away; but then he 'laid the paper down and set there thinking . . . And went on thinking. And got to thinking over our trip down the river; and I see Jim before me, all the time, in the day, and in the night-time, sometimes moonlight, sometimes storms, and we a floating along, talking, and singing, and laughing.' There is more of this, but the quotation will suggest the extraordinary intensity of emotion together with the convincing representation in words of the free flow of reminiscence and emotion, devoid of the artifices of official rhetoric, undisciplined by syntax (although cunningly controlled in rhythm), and over-whelmingly concrete: a torrent of emotionally charged images.

The Huck who could not harden himself against Jim is the 'real' or 'true' Huck, the boy who has, as Mark Twain said when he described the book ten years later, a 'sound heart.' The depraved conscience is unreal; it is an intrusion from without, just as the Duke and the King on the raft are invaders from the shore, and its threat is overcome. The narrator of the story, looking back over his experiences, knows that he has been victorious in his struggle with his conscience. The remembered struggle merely lends richness and depth to his character, Basically this character is natural man, pure and spontaneously good. But we must remember the pattern of values Mark Twain has established for his story: the contrast between the River and the Shore. Huck's goodness has to be defined in opposition to the standards of propriety and respectability that prevail in organised society. He is the Bad Boy – he is dirty and ungrammatical, he steals chickens and watermelons, he is an accomplished liar, he runs away and lives a vagabond existence with an escaped slave. In the moral system of the novel, these traits of the Bad Boy simply establish his innocence and purity. It is a scheme having something in common with the heart-of-gold formula popularised by Bret Harte, but more profound because much more serious, more deeply felt by the author. □

This is a definitive account of the Huck who struggles with his conscience over Jim, and of the terms of that struggle. It is supplemented in a footnote by Smith's reference to Twain's Notebook entry, ten years after *Huckleberry Finn* was published, in which Twain refers to the novel as 'a book of mine where a sound heart & a deformed conscience come into collision & conscience suffers defeat'. Whether we can separate the real from the unreal Huck as clearly as Smith insists remains a matter for endless debate. Why is someone who believes in slavery not real? Moreover, Twain gives sound-hearted Huck no endorsement. Whatever commitment to Jim this Huck makes, in chapters 16 and 31, is deeply packaged in irony and always aborted by what follows. Smith talks about 'the narrator of the story, looking back over his experiences', but if by narrator he means Huck, there is no sign that Huck has arrived anywhere from which to look back. The journey is going nowhere both physically and metaphysically. As we leave the novel, there is no sign that Huck has learned anything, except that he does not want to return to where he has been. All he knows is that he wants to move on, but to what? It is as if the past, humiliating or corrupting as it has been, has already exhausted the future.

As Smith moves towards his conclusion, he discusses Huck as narrative persona for Twain. 'Huck Finn is the literary culmination of [the] deadpan manner. Through Mark Twain's use of Huck as narrator he is able to wear the mask of innocence.' Smith finds more consistency in

Huck's innocence than is justified, especially as many of Huck's schemes are based on considerable worldly knowledge and, in Smith's words, 'his memory is stored with images of violence and calamity, bereavement, sickness, separation of families, and especially of boys left alone in the world by the death of parents.' With this knowledge, innocence could only be a mask for Huck as well as Twain.

We are getting close to appreciating that Huck is the mask for a variety of authorial positions and responses as much as it is the name for a consistent character. His vernacular may look and sound the same, but at different moments it may imply a different identity, a different kind of consciousness, sometimes innocent, sometimes as cynical as ever the Duke can be. As Smith points out, he is not 'capable of arriving at the abstract proposition, "Slavery is wrong"'. This incapacity for moral development, which will be returned to later, is related to the nihilism Smith eventually finds in *Huckleberry Finn*:

■ In the course of this novel the alienation from society that is hinted at in Colonel Sherburn's speech is established as the author's dominant attitude. The major direction of his thought thereafter takes him with increasing bitterness through 'The Man That Corrupted Hadleyburg' and *Pudd'nhead Wilson* to *The Mysterious Stranger*. In this fable Satan symbolically destroys the image of Hannibal which was Mark Twain's persistent metaphor for human society. The later books enable us to recognise that the contrast in *Huckleberry Finn* between the River and the Shore contains a latent anarchism and even nihilism. □

Related to this nihilism, is 'the tendency toward primitivism' that is implicit in *Huckleberry Finn*.

By now Smith has joined forces with Rahv:

■ The vernacular style greatly limited the power of Mark Twain and his successors to deal with abstract thought and thus has fostered anti-intellectualism. The repudiation of the Western European literary tradition, while in one sense a liberation for the writer, cuts him off from the accumulated experience of the past and commits him to the often wasteful enterprise of building from the ground up. Mark Twain's career, with its false starts and its lack of continuity, reveals the disadvantages as well as the advantages of the literary pioneer. Like the actual pioneer, he had to pay a high price for his conquest of new territory, and his debt was entailed upon his heirs. □

A.E. Dyson[8] returns us again to the ending of the novel. Implicitly his reading is a challenge to Smith's bipolar thesis. In his view critical dissatisfaction with the ending is related to

■ . . . the very common error of regarding the novel as a simple con-trast between *two* worlds – the one civilised, insensitive and corrupt, the other uncivilised, sensitive and humane. The widow, 'dismal regular and decent' as Huck calls her, is seen as typical of the former: Huck himself and Jim as typical of the latter. Tom Sawyer, whilst having many fine qualities, belongs basically to the widow's world; and Twain's irony is taken to be the playing off of the genuine against the conventional, the good, if one likes, against the bad.

Now though this is true in that the values achieved on the raft are used for an ironic survey of society at large, I am convinced that to put the matter so simply is misleading. For one thing it overlooks, as most criticism does, the importance of the Duke, the King, and Huck's father. These are all far further away from the 'respectable' folk than Huck himself is; yet they are the most decisively evil characters in the book. One has only to recall them to be aware that Jim stands less hope of mercy from this group than he does from Miss Watson and Tom, and that a straight choice of 'outsider' against 'insider' is not at all what is being presented. Nor is this all. The eventual freeing of Jim comes about not through the journey on the raft, but through a change of heart in his former owner. The method by which it happens is muddled, the insights behind it are less pure, to put the matter mildly, than those of the raft, yet the fact of freedom comes from Miss Watson's dying request, and from the camp of the respectable. In allowing this, Mark Twain is not 'selling out' the rest of the novel, as some commentators assume, but simply being faithful to the realism which makes us trust him all along. Respectable morality, though muddled and sometimes cruel, does have certain ideals behind it: the ideals, indeed, which Huck himself embodies in a purer form, outside society, and paradoxically in defiance of it. The world of the widow and of Miss Watson might be blinkered and provided with blind eyes for all occasions; it might recoil with horror from its own more Christian ideals when despite every precaution it accidentally catches sight of them; but it is myopic rather than totally blind, thoughtlessly rather than wilfully cruel. Miss Watson's request in her will is the beginning, maybe, of a challenge to the system of slavery from inside: a moment without which no purer moral protest, however noble, would stand much hope of eventually winning the majority to its side. If we think historically, we shall see that her dying decision to free Jim, despite the fact that he has sinned both against herself and against the economic system by escaping, may be as important a land-mark on the road to emancipation as the dangerous quest for freedom on the raft itself. Actual humane progress does come about, whether we like it or not, through muddled insights, muddled kindliness, muddled actions as much as from the straightforward vindication of ideals. Twain's ending draws attention to this, too, and it is also part of the whole truth he has to tell. □

Dyson is right to see that the Duke, the King and Huck's father cannot be identified with society. They themselves are a challenge to society's laws and conventions, which they exploit. To be at odds with society, therefore, is not in itself commendable. But are these three 'the most decisively evil characters in the book'? Is anyone evil in *Huckleberry Finn*? Eventually Huck, in the opening lines of chapter 18, is humorously resigned to his father, and when the Duke and the King are the victims of a mob in chapter 33 we have this famous moment: 'Well, it made me sick to see it; and I was sorry for them poor pitiful rascals, it seemed like I couldn't ever feel any hardness against them any more in the world'. Twain hated mobs. He feared both finding himself in one and finding himself pursued by one. How can we be sure we are saved from either fate? Dyson replaces the simplification he is attacking with one of his own. Like previous readers he misses all the comedy in the presentation of Pap, the Duke and the King, for example in those wonderfully funny and vivid paragraphs at the end of chapter 5, detailing Pap's dealings with the new judge. The balance of the narrator's and the author's support undoubtedly comes down on Pap's side in this episode. He is the agent for the sort of pillorying of sentimental gentility Twain has enjoyed since such an early piece as 'The Story of the Bad Little Boy'. Similarly, Twain relishes the language of the Duke and the King in chapter 19, as they describe how they get a living:

■ I done considerable in the doctoring way in my time. Layin' on o' hands is my best holt – for cancer and paralysis, and sich things; and I k'n tell a fortune pretty good, when I've got somebody along to find out the facts for me. Preachin's my line, too; and workin' camp-meetin's; and missionaryin' around. □

Dyson is on firmer ground in appreciating the realistic implications of Miss Watson's conversion, though his attention to it is out of proportion to Twain's interest in it.

As the title of her essay indicates, Millicent Bell[9] sees the ending of the novel as a confirmation of its mood throughout. Referring to Leo Marx's thesis that Twain botched his masterpiece with the ending, Bell writes:

■ It seems possible, however, that Twain's narrative is not moulded so intentionally and does not betray itself in its conclusion. Huck himself is without conscious sense of goal most of the time, and, after Cairo has been passed, freedom for Jim becomes a forgotten enterprise.

Perhaps the major figure, that of a raft borne downstream not by the conscious will of the men on board but by impersonal natural forces, suggests Huck's passivity in ordering his experiences, giving significance to the adventures which come to him by the flow of time. No work may be more existential, perhaps, than this one, which seems to exhibit its hero as submitting to a process by which the self, far from seeking and attaining new forms, is subjected to a perilous sequence of breakdowns. The reiterated motif of death, often noticed, suggests how close, repeatedly, Huck comes to loss of the self, how negative a condition is the freedom he experiences. That a positive new self might be gained in the place of what is lost is hardly envisaged by Twain. □

Forgetting Jim, Bell concentrates on Huck. Eventually, his passivity and negativity lead to his being re-identified as Tom Sawyer:

■ And it is symbolically appropriate that it is Tom that he is taken to be, now. When he realises this, he is ready to relapse, with relief, into that role which is so much the easier one, to give up the terrible burden, morally speaking, the awful isolation from the rest of his world, of being Huckleberry Finn. In this light we can respond to his remark. 'Well, it was like being born again, I was so glad to find out who I was.'

Literally, of course, he is merely expressing relief at discovering who he has been taken for, which is, to discover that he has an identity, however false, which he can perfectly enact, since it belongs to his familiar old friend. But the relief is more meaningful than this. He is reborn again into Tom Sawyer's world, into the sense of adventures uninvolved with those taxing dilemmas, those crises of being, which his Huckleberry Finn adventures have involved. 'Being Tom Sawyer was easy and comfortable.' Being Huckleberry Finn has been difficult precisely because it has involved, all along the journey, such nearly fatal losses of identity' as represented by the passage quoted above from chapter XXXII.

In an immediate sense, the Phelps Farm episode – despite the final promise to 'light out' – effects what James M. Cox called Huck's 'sad initiation' into his society. Perhaps it is as reactionary and as inferior artistically to the rest as Leo Marx charged it with being. But it should be recognized that the conformist self, represented by Tom Sawyer, is internally present in Huck, though Tom is absent between the opening and the closing of the book. From the Tom side of himself Huck partly, painfully breaks free, but such rejections are never complete. The Tom side remains, takes over again. The conflict is resolved in a way that is not false to experience, for what Huck has nearly rejected is not merely cruelty and greed; along with St Petersburg respectability, he has rejected all social roles.

Dying to older selves we run the risk of failing to find new modes of being in the world of living men. We have surrendered, without replacing, those memberships of caste and class and race, those attitudes by which one is defined in the interlocking design of social relationships. The simpler harmony of the child with his world is available only in memory and reached for by Twain as nostalgically as Proust would reach for the lost paradise of Illers. The idealised white town of *Tom Sawyer* has become a ramshackle Bricksville, where the finest gentleman shoots down the town drunk in cold blood. But things have not really changed so much as they have always been this way, Twain realised, having known of such a murder in Hannibal. To reject this blackened world altogether is to face the outer dark of the loss of all community and of the self that can only subsist in community. To think otherwise, Twain may have believed, is to imagine that Utopia, the condition of the raft afloat upon its mystic river, can continue ashore. □

Realistically, who can live in what Bell terms 'the awful isolation' – not Cooper's Ishmael Bush in *The Prairie*, not Poe's Roderick Usher, not Melville's Captain Ahab, not the Whitman of 'I saw in Louisiana a live-oak growing'? In nineteenth century American literature there may need to be a settling for an inherited identity, even if such an identity can be no more than implied. American novels and poems, no matter how formally radical, must themselves accept their generic designation and their complicity with all previous novels and poems, all previous literature. In a 'little one-horse town' in Arkansas (Ch.21) Shakespeare makes his presence felt, even though only about twelve people turn up for the show.

For Bell, Huck is relieved to be Tom Sawyer; for Leland Krauth[10] he is 'Mark Twain's version of the eighteenth century Man of Feeling'. As Krauth joins the struggle to get a fix on Twain's most famous narrator, he is clearly moving in the opposite direction to praising Huck as an embodiment of the frontier spirit, uncorrupted by civilisation. Initially Krauth makes his point by rehearsing the influence of Southwestern humour on Twain. As he sees it, 'Four elements of *Huckleberry Finn* have been singled out as particularly common to the tradition of Southwestern humour: the con-men (the Duke and the King), the camp meeting, the circus, and the Royal Nonesuch'. But Twain's presentation of these traditional motifs is significantly different from the way they are treated by other Southwestern humorists. Krauth concentrates on the camp meeting as a case in point:

■ Camp meetings were of course both realities of backwoods life and stock episodes in the humorous fiction that fastened onto that life. The differences between Twain's camp meeting and that of Johnson Jones Hooper in *Some Adventures of Captain Simon Suggs*, the literary work most often cited as a source, illustrate how Twain Victorianizes the tradition of Southwestern humour. Hooper's camp meeting is at once an orgy, a fleecing, a thrill-filled happening, and a staged melodrama. The religious longings presumably informing the meeting are transparently bogus; the impulses that actually animate the gathering are sexual, monetary, sensational, and theatrical. Hooper is insistent upon the sensual aspect of the action. 'Men and women,' he writes, 'rolled about on the ground, or lay sobbing or shouting in promiscuous heaps.' He exposes the sexual urgencies underlying the crowd's frenzy in a highly suggestive language:

'Keep the thing warm!' roared a sensual seeming man, of stout mould and florid countenance, who was exhorting among a bevy of young women, upon whom he was lavishing caresses. 'Keep the thing warm, breethring! – come to the Lord, honey!' he added, as he vigorously hugged one of the damsels he sought to save.

'*Gl-o-ree!*' yelled a huge . . . woman, as in a fit of the jerks, she threw herself convulsively from her feet, and fell like a thousand of brick across a diminutive old man in a little round hat, who was squeaking consolation to one of the mourners.

'Good Lord, have mercy!' ejaculated the little man.

In his punning Hooper is daring as well as amusing. He writes here very much in the so-called strong masculine vein of Southwestern humour.

In his camp meeting Twain preserves the sense of the meeting's monetary, sensational, and theatrical impulses, but he all but eliminates the sexual. Huck gives us this description:

The women had on sun-bonnets; and some had linsey-woolsey frocks, some gingham ones, and a few of the young ones had on calico. Some of the young men was barefooted, and some of the children didn't have on any clothes but just a tow-linen shirt. Some of the old women was knitting, and some of the young folks was courting on the sly.

This is far from the sexual antics of Hooper's fanatics, and it is far indeed from his ribald language. In fact, Huck's acknowledgement of covert play between the sexes is phrased in such a way as to suggest its essential innocence: 'the young folks was courting on the sly.'

Twain does come somewhat closer to the sensual when he has Huck describe the crowd's response to the King's outlandish tale of conversion from piracy to missionary work, but again a transformation of the raw material of Southwestern humour is apparent:

> So the King went all through the crowd with his hat, swabbing his eyes and blessing the people and praising them and thanking them for being so good to the poor pirates away off there; and every little while the prettiest kind of girls, with the tears running down their cheeks, would up and ask him would he let them kiss him, for to remember him by: and he always done it; and some of them he hugged and kissed as many as five or six times.

The King is a bit of a lecher, though finally more interested in cash than kissing, and the young girls could be said to be sublimating their sexual urges, but what Twain invites us to laugh at them for is not their sublimated desires but their misplaced sentimentality.

Twain's expurgation of the traditional camp meeting is representative of the way he Victorianizes the material of Southwestern humour. He effects similar changes in presenting his con men, the circus, and the *Royal Nonesuch* – his version of Gyascutus, that favourite exhibition of Southwestern lewdness. (Huck says the performance was enough to make 'a cow laugh' but he characteristically declines to describe it.) In discussing Twain's ties to George Washington Harris (Harris of course creates a camp meeting that is almost as lascivious as Hooper's), one critic has suggested that they share a sense of 'man's predisposition to dehumanise himself.'[11] But more often than not in *Huckleberry Finn* Twain refuses to let his characters debase themselves by being the fully carnal, somewhat bestial creatures of their tradition. □

Krauth's conclusion is that 'Twain purges from the Southwestern tradition its exuberant celebration of rough and tumble masculinity'. The reason for this purgation is that the novel is replete with the fear of masculine violence:

■ The book is surcharged with an atmosphere of imminent violence whose source is simply the nature of white males. The ferocity they embody erupts in the antics of Pap, in the search of the slave hunters, in the feud between the Grangerfords and Shepherdsons, in the relationship of the Duke and the King, in the mob that rides them out of town on a rail, and in the acts of the *Walter Scott* gang, as well as in the gunning down of Boggs. The terror of this masculine violence is intensified by its arbitrariness. When Huck is seeking information about Cairo the day after he has fooled the pair of slave hunters, he meets a nameless man setting a trotline from his skiff. Their encounter is emblematic of the male world of the novel:

> 'Mister, is that Cairo?'
> 'Cairo? no. You must be a blame' fool.'
> 'What town is it, mister?'
> 'If you want to know, go and find out. If you stay here botherin' around me for about a half a minute longer, you'll get something you won't want.'

Twain's imagination seems haunted by the memory of a gratuitous hostility in men that borders on violence. The memory is partly of literature, of the rough men who people Southwestern humour, but it is also a recollection of life, of his life in Hannibal, on the river, and in the West. And no doubt this image of man has something to do with the father, John Marshall Clemens, the Judge and Southern gentleman of whom Mark Twain once secretly recorded: 'Silent, austere, of perfect probity and high principle; ungentle of manner toward his children, but always a gentleman in his phrasing – and never punished them – a look was enough, and more than enough.' Although Twain is sixty-two when he makes this notation, the remembrance of fear is still strong – 'a look was enough, and more than enough.' Hamlin Hill has recently suggested that 'fear' was in fact 'the controlling emotion' of Mark Twain's life.[12] Certainly fear is the dominant emotion in Huck Finn's experience, and it is most often a fear engendered by the men of his world (Huck is never afraid of women). □

In contrast to these masculine tendencies, we have what is embodied in Huck. According to Krauth, he has the qualities of a Mississippi steamboat pilot, as registered by Twain in a letter: 'the only real, independent & genuine *gentlemen* in the world go quietly up & down the Mississippi river, asking no homage of anyone, seeking no popularity, no notoriety, & not caring a damn whether school keeps or not'.[13] Huck too, in Krauth's words,

■ . . . goes quietly down the Mississippi, asking 'no homage of any one, seeking no popularity, no notoriety, & not caring a damn whether school keeps or not.' It is no accident that when Huck struggles with his conscience, tying to bring himself to turn Jim in, Twain specifically has Huck denounce himself for his failure to do the 'right' thing in the language of manhood. 'I warn't,' Huck says, 'man enough – hadn't the spunk of a rabbit.' On the contrary, of course, in resisting the pressures of his society, the norms that dictate Jim's return to slavery, Huck demonstrates not only his freedom but also his true manhood. Like the pilot of Twain's vision, Huck assays above the multitude in genuine manliness. His fortitude in determining to free Jim at whatever cost to himself stands in stark contrast to the self-vaunting courage of the other white males of the novel – and of their prototypes in previous Southwestern humour. Twain recreates the hero of that tradition in Huck, replacing the aggressive, violent male with a passive, loving one. Further, through Jim, Twain ascribes to Huck an additional status. As a recent critic has pointed out, a number of 'labels' are imposed on Huck, none of which fits the reality of his character.[14] Thus to the Widow Douglas he is a 'poor lost lamb', and to Pap he is 'a good deal of a big-bug', while to Miss Watson he is simply a 'fool.'

Only Jim, who comes to know Huck intimately on the raft, really apprehends the essence of Huck's character. He articulates for us the significance of Huck. On the most intimate level, Huck is 'de ole true Huck,' Jim's 'bes' fren,' but Huck is for Jim also something more: he is a 'white genlman.'

Huck is the true man and gentleman of the novel, Twain's most radical departure from the tradition that nurtured him. Before Twain the gentleman was trapped in the frame of the Southwestern tale, reduced to moralising about the action in polite language, while the free and the manly were represented by the unfeeling, amoral, violent vulgarians of the story itself.[15] □

From Jim's 'white genlman' he becomes Krauth's 'eighteenth century Man of Feeling'. We, however, may be more fascinated by the aspects of *Huckleberry Finn* highlighted by Krauth than we are convinced by his thesis. We may also feel some loss of realism on Twain's part in his purgation of the Southwestern tradition, though remnants of this tradition may remain in Huck's ungentlemanly identification of one of the Wilks sisters as 'the hare-lip'. Like many critics before him, Krauth cites Huck's attempts in chapter 13 to help the *Walter Scott* gang as evidence of Huck's virtuous pre-disposition, but he omits any reference to the complicating ironies of Huck's last pronouncements on this episode:

■ 'But take it all around, I was feeling ruther comfortable on accounts of taking all this trouble for that gang, for not many would a done it. I wished the widow knowed about it. I judged she would be proud of me for helping these rapscallions, because rapscallions and dead beats is the kind the widow and the good people takes the most interest in.' □

If the widow's good works on behalf of dead beats can be treated sarcastically, why cannot Huck's? In any case he is ready with his humorously cynical self-defence, when he suspects his efforts have been to no avail:

'I felt a little bit heavy-hearted about the gang, but not much, for I reckoned if they could stand it, I could.' Huck cannot always be identified with the qualities Krauth finds in him. Even after all he has experienced with Jim, he can finally say: 'I knowed he was white inside.'

The impossibility of understanding Huck as a traditionally consistent character is one of the issues addressed by Stuart Hutchinson.[16] Hutchinson begins by contrasting *Huckleberry Finn* with *Tom Sawyer*. In the latter there is 'rhetorical extravagance' in the account of Injun Joe's death, 'because heavy themes are injected into a novel too light to carry them':

■ The measure of the superiority of *Huckleberry Finn* over *Tom Sawyer* is that it can always bear Twain's profoundest concerns. Evidence of this resilience appears as early as the last two paragraphs of Chapter 1, when Huck feels 'so lonesome I most wished I was dead'. Eventually, *Huckleberry Finn* will demolish Hamlet's 'To be, or not to be' soliloquy, 'the most celebrated thing in Shakespeare' (Ch.21). This literal deconstruction, however, follows the construction of an American equivalent to the soliloquy in these early paragraphs.

Like *Hamlet*, *Huckleberry Finn* will respond variously to death. The morbid Emmeline Grangerford's drawings and poems, and the sublime Icing's claim that the dead Peter Wilks in his coffin, 'lays yonder, cold but joyful' (Ch.25), are but two of the responses. At the end of Chapter 1 Huck, like Hamlet in the soliloquy, is both tempted and oppressed by death. Neither the physical nor metaphysical world seems capable of consoling revelation. The stars shine; the leaves rustle; the wind whispers; a restless ghost grieves in the woods.

Obviously, the Huck equipped with such a sensibility is not the innocent boy traditionally seen as the central figure of the novel. Huck has a number of functions for Twain, and to be an innocent boy is only one of them. He is best seen as the equivalent of Whitman's 'I' in 'Song of Myself' and *Leaves of Grass* generally. He is the enactment of a number of versions of the authorial self, responding to that self's formative American world. Sometimes Huck is innocent or unconscious of the implications of what he is saying. Sometimes he is neither.

How, for example, are we to read the second sentence of the first of the paragraphs I am referring to: 'By-and-by they fetched the niggers in and had prayers, and then everybody went off to bed'? This sentence could be ironic, in the sense that a reader's consciousness of slavery is aroused by the narrator's unconscious acceptance of it. Alternatively, the sentence could express the narrator's brooding, guilty consciousness of slavery, similar to Quentin Compson's in *The Sound and the Fury*. Like the whole book, the paragraphs are written in the past tense. As always in *Huckleberry Finn*, however, we have no sense of the present to which this past has led. There is no end from which narrator, author, or reader can get a fix on any moment of the narrator's past life. In common with other works of the nineteenth century American literature, the only end *Huckleberry Finn* recognises is death. There is no end on the way to *the* end, such as is offered in nineteenth century English novels. There is no resolving plot.

However it is read, the sentence about the niggers confesses the narrator's corruption. In other words, the sensibility enacted in *Huckleberry Finn* can be representative and tragic, because, like Hamlet's it is inevitably complicit in the sullied world from which it strives to be free. □

Huckleberry Finn contrasts with the English and thoroughly plotted *Great Expectations* in that we have no sense of the end from which the narrator is telling his story. This means there could never have been a resolving plot. Not surprisingly, therefore, when one is mentioned in the first paragraph of chapter 15, it is quickly forgotten. With this paragraph Twain, in Hutchinson's words, gives us

■ one kind of book. It is recognized Huck and Jim could have headed for the 'free States'. *Huckleberry Finn*, however, is always becoming another kind of book.

This other kind of book realises and explores the range of Twain's South-Western culture, as a representative expression of the human condition. Rather than enacting a cause and effect plot, Huck's adventures enable the realisation and the exploration. Like the representative son in Sophocles' trilogy, Huck, wanting only to leave trouble behind, sets out on a journey on which his life, to say the least, never gets any better. This is why the raft goes South – because in the profoundest sense, humankind has nowhere else to go, other than where it is. □

The Grangerfords are one example of the range of experience Huck encounters. In his response to this episode Hutchinson begins with the first paragraph of chapter 18:

■ In this paragraph's description of Colonel Grangerford the powerful, elemental forces realised in the major characters in *Huckleberry Finn* are again apparent. I am thinking of 'the blackest kind of eyes, sunk so deep back that they seemed like they was looking out of caverns at you', and the 'lightening' that can 'flicker out' from these eyes. The paragraph ends:

Everybody loved to have him around, too; he was sunshine most always – I mean he made it seem like good weather. When he turned into a cloud bank it was awful dank for half a minute and that was enough; there wouldn't nothing go wrong again for a week.

What keeps these god-like forces under control is extreme self-repression and an exacting performance as a gentleman. The repression is indicated by the repetition in the paragraph of the words 'thin' and 'thinnest'. The performance requires the daily costume of 'a clean shirt and full suit from head to foot made out of linen so white it hurt your eyes to look at it'.

Like James with Gilbert Osmond in *The Portrait of a Lady*, Twain, with Colonel Grangerford, and later with Colonel Sherburn, shows how a way of life may never come naturally to an American self. Identity is a continuing act. Introducing Osmond in Chapter 22, James writes: 'he was a gentleman who studied style'. This judgement might be made of either of the two colonels in *Huckleberry Finn*.

Yet Huck makes a more enlivening remark, at least about Colonel Grangerford; 'He was a gentleman all over; and so was his family'. This delightful comment and the description that follows project more potentiality into Colonel Grangerford than ever Osmond has. Osmond is rather finished off by James, even in the introduction to him. There is not in him, as there is in Colonel Grangerford, that complexity of fundamental energies, which participates in, and contributes to, the essential contradictions of our existence. Demonstrably, *Huckleberry Finn* is made up of greater forces than a James novel. In Colonel Grangerford's case, whatever is in the caverns behind his eyes finds final expression in a fight to the death with a clan exactly like his own.

This feud, the first cause of which no one can remember, is exemplary human conflict. It is not presented so that we can simply mock the participants, as if the Grangerfords and Shepherdsons were the only people on earth to listen to sermons about brotherly love and then kill one another. Because no amount of wisdom and love has ever eradicated such killing, Huck himself cannot escape a representative complicity in it: 'I reckoned I was to blame, somehow'. The dead Buck, 'laying in the edge of the water' (Ch.18), could as well be a dead Huck, just as any of the thousands of dead bodies we see on our screens could as well be any of us. No plot saves us from such a fate. □

According to Hutchinson, human contradictions are reproduced in the elements themselves. During the thunderstorm in chapter 9 natural energy suggests the descriptive terms, 'lovely', 'wild', 'glory', and 'sin'. Hutchinson next turns to the Huck who in chapters 16 and 31 wrestles with his conscience about Jim. On each of these occasions, Huck shows signs of a development which Twain immediately aborts. In Hutchinson's view,

■ Twain has indeed an investment in not allowing Huck to develop the moral sense, which might decide slavery is wrong, and which might be associated with a journey towards an end. In what has become a well-known notebook entry of August 1895, he described *Huckleberry Finn* as, 'a book of mine where a sound heart and a deformed conscience come into collision and conscience suffers defeat'. With this observation in mind, we may see Huck, at the crucial moments in Chapters 16 and 31, as an expression of 'sound-heart' and 'deformed-conscience'. I hyphenate these terms, because, as enacted in *Huckleberry Finn*, they are the equivalent of composite nouns. In Chapters 16 and 31, when Huck is trying to work out whether his commitment to Jim is good or bad, his heart cannot be other than sound, nor his conscience other than deformed.

He does right, but cannot think right. At these junctures his condition is the reverse of what is normally human. Our moral sense may allow us to think right, but it cannot guarantee we do right. Later works by Twain, especially *The Mysterious Stranger*, reveal how enraged he was by the frequent impotence, or self-contradictory results, of moral sense. He felt humiliated by the 'Shadow' which, in Eliot's words from 'The Hollow Men', so often falls 'Between the idea/ And the reality'. One of the Hucks in the book, therefore, will by-pass the complications and contradictions of moral sense. Endowed with the incorruptible and intuitive goodness of a sound-heart this Huck, in crisis over Jim, will do good, even though deformed-conscience tells him it is bad. This Huck, moreover, will journey nowhere, because he will never be allowed to develop from the innocence of being unable to recognise his own virtue.

Not that this is a position Twain can rest on, even though he is attracted to it. As in all great books, the authorial imagination in *Huckleberry Finn* is always turned critically on any thesis it advances. In Chapters 16 and 31, therefore, readers may think right with respect to Jim and slavery, even though Huck cannot. Moral development, withheld from the narrator, is allowed to us. The humour of this irony gives us a position of superiority over Huck, and qualifies the author's commitment to Huck's sound-heart. Twain cannot maintain an uncritical faith in the absoluteness of intuition, not even in the intuition of the nineteenth century's Romantic child. If Huck's 'doing whichever come handiest at the time' (Ch.16) could lead to a life in harmony with nature aboard the raft, it could equally result in the degradation and destitution embodied in Pap. Worst of all, freedom from moral sense could become wilful and lead to Colonel Sherburn's gunning down of Boggs.

Even Miss Watson's deathbed remorse can be seen as a critique both of Huck's innocence of moral sense with respect to slavery, and also of the book's fundamental disbelief in development. Miss Watson gives Jim freedom; Huck gets him nowhere. She eventually recognises she has been wrong. In a very minor key, hers is the moral development of many of literature's heroines and heroes. She has what George Eliot in Chapter 54 of *Daniel Deronda* terms 'a root of conscience'. It is what we traditionally rely on for the recognition and rectification of evil. The presupposition is that the moral sense complicit in evil can, with the aid of conscience, transform itself and conquer evil.

The adventures do not achieve an end, because Twain has no faith in this presupposition, even though he can acknowledge in Miss Watson its contribution to human affairs, Equally, as we have seen, he can acknowledge a book which would have taken Huck and Jim 'among the free States'. *Huckleberry Finn* is plural in its sense of possibility. Twain's own view of conscience, however, is voiced by Huck, when he discovers what several of Twain's voices in other books also discover:

> it don't make no difference whether you do right or wrong, a person's conscience ain't got no sense, and just goes for him *anyway*. If I had a yaller dog that didn't know no more than a person's conscience does, I would pison him. It takes up more room than all the rest of a person's insides, and yet ain't no good, nohow. Tom Sawyer he says the same. (Ch.33)

Traditionally, conscience is as the voice of God. Here, it becomes not even 'Godot', but is reversed to dog.

The adventures achieve no end, because *Huckleberry Finn* claims no access to a transcendent morality, according to which the human condition might be improved. . . .

But the book is not saying the great evil of slavery cannot be eradicated. There are 'free States'; slave owners like Miss Watson can be converted; readers of the book, experiencing Huck's contortions of conscience, may be convinced of slavery's Preposterousness; on the raft there can be absolute equality. All these possibilities hold true, yet the evil and injustice of the world remain a constant quantity, no matter which instances are remedied. In *Huckleberry Finn*, Twain wants to confirm particular possibilities of arrival, while maintaining the sense of a journey without destination through unchanging conditions. □

But what about Jim, seen not from Huck's point of view, but considered as a character in his own right? Before continuing with Hutchinson on this matter, it is appropriate to widen the context of the debate. Arlin

Turner[17] argues for the influence of George Washington Cable on *Huckleberry Finn*. Cable's novels *The Grandissimes* (1880) and *Madame Delphine* (1881) had vividly depicted Creole life in Civil War New Orleans, where Cable was born, and had dealt with black/white relations and the problems arising from the exploitation of black people. According to Turner,

■ In *Life on the Mississippi* and elsewhere Mark Twain praised Cable's literary work, and he had great respect for the courage, the devotion, and the logical argument Cable brought to his campaign for Negro rights. Although Mark Twain did not join in the public debate, there can be little doubt that Cable influenced his thought on Southern issues from the early 1880s onward. That influence can be detected at a few points in *Life on the Mississippi*, especially in portions omitted from the book as printed, and in progressively larger portions in *Huckleberry Finn*, in the sections on slavery in *A Connecticut Yankee in King Arthur's Court*, and in *Pudd'nhead Wilson*. It has been plausibly argued that Cable was largely responsible for the fact that *Huckleberry Finn* became, not a proper sequel to *Tom Sawyer*, as first intended, but instead a probing of human character and social institutions, particularly those relating to slavery.

Huckleberry Finn was a book to please Cable, and Mark Twain read from its pages when they appeared on the platform together in the winter of 1884–85. The climactic episode of the book brings Huck Finn into a 'close place,' where he must decide whether to report Jim, a runaway slave or to continue helping Jim toward freedom, and in doing so to violate the laws of man and, he believes, the laws of God. When he decides, finally, to tear up the letter he has written to report Jim, and says, 'All right, then, I'll go to hell,' slave society stands under indictment, and along with it the doctrines of race which had bolstered up the institution of slavery. Thus the indictment applied to American society in 1884 no less than in the slave era which had closed two decades earlier. Whether the impetus came from Cable or other sources, *Huckleberry Finn* made the fullest attack Mark Twain had yet written on any element in his Southern heritage. □

Turner continues:

■ In spite of Jim's presence, however, and the danger that he may be returned to his owner, slavery is seen only obliquely; not slavery but slave doctrine is presented. The view reflected in Pap Finn's drunken tirade against a government which allows a 'white-shirted free nigger' to vote in the state across the river has no focus on a slave or slave conditions, and time distortion which the slave society has produced in Pap Finn's mind is one of the lesser aberrations he has suffered. If the reader is aware of slavery, finally, he recalls Huck's heroism in risking damnation to hell to help his friend: or he remembers the harmless Phelpses, who in righteous innocence accept chattel slavery as ordained of God. The author's main concern is not to reveal or even to suggest the plight of the slaves: it is rather to expose the folly and the dishonesty underlying the prevailing doctrines on race. In this regard the book has few equals. It elaborates in fiction some of the views written out for the late chapters of *Life on the Mississippi* but deleted before the book was printed. These views could have come directly from George W. Cable, as could also the condemnation in another deleted passage of the solid white vote in the South.

Huckleberry Finn paints the world of the lower Mississippi as the whites see it. To be sure, Huck's level of social vision is little above Jim's, but his sympathy for Jim is inconstant and may seem to imply an identification which does not exist. The white man's doctrine of race superiority is held up to ridicule, but the victim of that doctrine remains unrealised. The basic situation, Huck and Jim raft-borne in flight before expected pursuers, led Mark Twain to formulate in this book a sequence of responses to the arguments on slavery and race he had known since childhood but had never before considered seriously. And even here the reader may get the impression that the sequence grew unawares to the author, while his attention was fixed on other elements.

But Mark Twain had long known that not every slave could expect to go rafting down the river to freedom; recollections extending back to his childhood furnished harsh proof to the contrary. He also knew that the doctrines of race which outlived slavery had far greater effects than to form queer ideas in the mind of a boy such as Huck. In 1874 he had published 'A True Story,' a short narrative telling that he once asked a Negro servant how she could have lived sixty years and 'never had any trouble.' She answered by recounting how in slave times her husband and seven children were sold away from her and how she met one son by accident during the Civil War. She concluded: 'Oh, no, Misto C – *I* hain't had no trouble. An' no Joy!' She thus places herself alongside Jim, a Negro employed to pass judgement on the white man's generalised view of race. But the story, in addition, hints that under suitable prompting the author might trace out the human effects of slavery and caste, and might draw full-scale characters in the process. □

The first two paragraphs above are another qualification of the centrality of Jim and slavery in *Huckleberry Finn*, while the account of 'A True Story' gives an accurate sense of Twain's earlier treatment of a black character.

Turner's account of Jim reminds us of one of Ralph Ellison's judgements about Jim: 'a white man's inadequate portrayal of a slave'. John H. Wallace confirms this judgement when he offers a response to the novel which may be taken by many black readers:

■ Ever since it was written, Mark Twain's *The Adventures of Huckleberry Finn* has provoked great controversy – and it runs on unabated even now in Fairfax County. After reading the book at least six times, I think it's perfectly all right for college class use, especially at the graduate level, where students can gain insight into the use and writing of satire and an uncensored flavour of the times. The caustic and abusive language is less likely to offend students of that age level because they tend to be mature enough to understand the ridicule.

Huckleberry Finn uses the pejorative term 'nigger' profusely. It speaks of black Americans with implications that they are not honest, they are not as intelligent as whites and they are not human. All of this, of course, is meant to be satirical. It is. But at the same time, it ridicules blacks. This kind of ridicule is extremely difficult for black youngsters to handle. I maintain that it constitutes mental cruelty, harassment and outright racial intimidation to force black students to sit in a classroom to read this kind of literature about themselves.

I read *Huck Finn* when I was in high school – and I can remember feeling betrayed by the teacher. I felt humiliated and embarrassed. Ten years ago, my oldest son went through the same experience in high school, until I went to talk to the teachers about it; and he lost all interest in English classes. Before reading this book, this bright energetic youngster was inquisitive and liked school; but afterward – after he had been asked to participate in the reading with an all-white class – I could see a definite negative change in his attitude toward teachers and school. (I'm happy to say he has recovered now.)

For years, black families have trekked to schools in just about every district in America to say that 'this book is bad for our children,' only to be turned away by insensitive and often unwittingly racist teachers and administrators responding that 'this is a classic.' Classic or not, it should not be allowed to continue to make our children feel bad about themselves.

I am convinced that the assignment and reading aloud of *Huck Finn* in our classrooms causes black children to have a low esteem of themselves and of their race. It also causes white students to have little or no respect for blacks. The resulting attitudes can lead to tension, discontent and fights. If the book is removed from the curriculums of our schools, there will be much better student-to-student, student-to-teacher and teacher-to-teacher relationships; and black students will definitely enjoy school a little bit more.

Every black child is the victim of the history of his race in this country. As John Fisher, former president of Columbia Teachers College has noted, 'On the day he enters kindergarten, he carries a burden no white child can ever know, no matter what handicaps or disabilities he may suffer.' Add to this the reading of a book like *Huckleberry Finn* and the experience can be devastatingly traumatic.

Many of my friends have cited First Amendment rights. But I am convinced that the continued use of pejorative materials about one particular racial group is a violation of the equal protection clause of the 14th Amendment. It also may violate the right to liberty as applied to reputation, in that the book maligns all black people.

I have no problem with *Huckleberry Finn* being on the library shelf, for any youngster or his parents to check out and read to their hearts' content, in school or at home. But, as a professional educator with 28 years of teaching at all levels, I cannot see the slightest need to use disparaging language to identify any racial, ethnic or religious group. If the lesson cannot be taught in positive terms, maybe it should not be taught.

We must be sensitive, creative teachers, encouraged to understand the special factors in the backgrounds of all the children – with curriculums that reflect these varied needs. And no sensitive, loving teacher would use *Huckleberry Finn* in class.

I am exceedingly shocked that *Time Post* has taken an editorial position that seventh-graders ought to be able to read the book in class. Many seventh- and eighth-graders have come to me and said they did not understand the language of the book, nor what it was about. Here, *The Post* misses a most salient point: that black students do not see the same thing in this book that a white teacher sees. We school administrators have to be selective and help our teachers use good judgement about their students and their teaching materials. That is a mandate from the state of Virginia that we must carry out.

Huckleberry Finn did not stand up to the scrutiny of two committees of experts: the human relations committee, made up of teachers and administrators, and a book review committee of teachers, administrators and parents. *Post* editors should take a closer look at the book and talk to black educators and students about its effect before blindly endorsing the use of this book by youngsters.[18] □

'Black students do not see the same thing in this book that a white teacher sees.' Such a comment returns us to the problems of audience raised at the beginning of the discussion of *Tom Sawyer*. One of the reasons nineteenth century American literature can be so formally unsettled is uncertainty about the identity of the audience it is addressing. Some very obvious divisions are white, black, American, English, and within all these divisions there is more than one sub-division. For example, a white racist and believer in the Biblical justification for slavery would presumably conclude Huck *would* go to hell for planning 'to steal Jim out of slavery again' in chapter 31. If Twain intends Huck's entire reflection at this moment to be ironical in the sense that Huck is good when he thinks he is bad, he cannot guarantee the irony will work for every reader. He has less control over it than Jane Austen has over the many ironies she delivers to her more homogeneous audience. In comparison to Twain she knows how to perform as author and her books know what to be, just as her characters know how to perform and, eventually, what to be. None of these conditions obtains for Twain, *Huckleberry Finn*, and Huck.

Turning more precisely to what Wallace sees as the racism in *Huckleberry Finn*, one kind of response to this view is offered by David L Smith.[19] His essay begins with a quotation from Thomas Jefferson:

■ They [blacks] are at least as brave, and more adventuresome [compared to whites]. But this may perhaps proceed from a want of fore-thought, which prevents their seeing a danger till it be present . . . They are more ardent after their female: but love seems with them to be more an eager desire, than a tender delicate mixture of sentiment and sensation. Their griefs are transient. Those numberless afflictions which render it doubtful whether heaven has given life to us in mercy or in wrath, are less felt, and sooner forgotten with them. In general, their existence appears to participate more of sensation than reflection. To this must be ascribed their disposition to sleep when abstracted from their diversions and unemployed in labor. □

Thomas Jefferson, *Notes on the State of Virginia* (187–8)

Almost any Euro-American intellectual of the nineteenth century could have written the preceding words. The notion of Negro inferiority was so deeply pervasive among those heirs of 'The Enlightenment' that the categories and even the vocabulary of Negro inferiority were formalised into a tedious, unmodulated litany. This uniformity increased rather than diminished during the course of the century. As Leon Litwack and others have shown, even the Abolitionists, who actively opposed slavery, frequently regarded blacks as inherently inferior. This helps to explain the widespread popularity of colonisation schemes among Abolitionists and other liberals.[20] As for Jefferson, it is not surprising that he held such ideas, but it is impressive that he formulated so clearly at the end of the eighteenth century what would become the dominant view of the Negro in the nineteenth century. In many ways, this Father of American Democracy – and quite possibly of five mulatto children – was a man of his time and ahead of his time.[21]

In July of 1876, exactly one century after the American Declaration of Independence, Mark Twain began writing *Adventures of Huckleberry Finn:* a novel which illustrates trenchantly the social limitations which American 'civilisation' imposes on individual freedom. The book takes special note of ways in which racism impinges upon the lives of Afro-Americans, even when they are legally 'free.' It is therefore ironic that *Huckleberry Finn* has often been attacked and even censored as a racist work. I would argue, on the contrary, that except for Melville's work, *Huckleberry Finn* is without peers among major Euro-American novels for its explicitly anti-racist stance. Those who brand the book 'racist' generally do so without having considered the specific form of racial discourse to which the novel responds. Furthermore, *Huckleberry Finn* offers much more than the typical liberal defences of 'human dignity' and protests against cruelty. Though it contains some such elements, it is more fundamentally a critique of those socially consti- tuted fictions – most notably romanticism, religion, and the concept of 'the Negro' – which serve to justify and to disguise selfish, cruel, and exploitative behaviour.

When I speak of 'racial discourse,' I mean more than simply attitudes about 'race' or conventions of talking about 'race.' Most importantly, I mean that 'race' itself is a discursive formation, which delimits social relations on the basis of alleged physical differences.[22] 'Race' is a strategy for relegating a segment of the population to a per- manent inferior status. It functions by insisting that each 'race' has specific, definitive, inherent behavioural tendencies and capacities, which distinguish it from other races. Though scientifically specious, 'race' has been powerfully effective as an ideology and as a form of social definition, which serves the interests of Euro-American hege- mony. In America, race has been deployed against numerous groups, including Native Americans, Jews, Asians, and even – for brief periods – an assortment of European immigrants.

For obvious reasons, however, the primary emphasis historically has been on defining 'the Negro' as a deviant from Euro-American norms. 'Race' in America means white supremacy and black inferior- ity[23] and 'the Negro', a socially constituted fiction, is a generalised, one-dimensional surrogate for the historical reality of Afro-American people. It is this reified fiction which Twain attacks in *Huckleberry Finn*.

Twain adopts a strategy of subversion in his attack on race. That is, he focuses on a number of commonplaces associated with 'the Negro,' and then he systematically dramatises their inadequacy. He uses the term 'nigger,' and he shows Jim engaging in superstitious behaviour. Yet he portrays Jim as a compassionate, shrewd, thoughtful, self-sacrificing and even wise man. Indeed, his portrayal of Jim contradicts every claim presented in Jefferson's description of 'the Negro.' Jim is cautious, he gives excellent advice, he suffers persistent anguish over separation from his wife and child and he even sacrifices his own sleep in order that Huck may rest.

Jim, in short, exhibits all the qualities that 'the Negro' supposedly lacks. Twain's conclusions do more than merely subvert the justifications of slavery, which was already long since abolished, Twain began this book during the final disintegration of Reconstruction, and his satire on antebellum Southern bigotry is also an implicit response to the Negro-phobic climate of the post-Reconstruction era.

It is troubling, therefore, that so many readers have completely misunderstood Twain's subtle attack on racism. Twain's use of the word 'nigger' has provoked some readers to reject the novel. As one of the most offensive words in our vocabulary, 'nigger' remains heavily shrouded in taboo. A careful assessment of this term within the context of American racial discourse, however, will allow us to understand the particular way in which the author uses it. If we attend closely to Twain's use of the word, we may find in it not just a trigger to outrage, but more importantly, a means of understanding the precise nature of American racism and Mark Twain's attack on it.

Most obviously, Twain uses 'nigger' throughout the book as a synonym for 'slave.' There is ample evidence from other sources that this corresponds to one usage common during the antebellum period. We first encounter it in reference to 'Miss Watson's big nigger named Jim' (Ch.2). This usage, like the term 'nigger stealer,' clearly designates the 'nigger' as a piece of property: a commodity, a slave. This passage also provides the only apparent textual justification for the common critical practice of labelling Jim, 'Nigger Jim,' as if 'nigger' were a part of his proper name. This loathsome habit goes back at least as far as Albert Bigelow Paine's biography of Twain (1912). In any case, 'nigger' in this sense connotes an inferior, even subhuman, creature, who is properly owned by and subservient to Euro-Americans.

Both Huck and Jim use the word in this sense. For example, when Huck fabricates his tale about the riverboat accident, the following exchange occurs between him and Aunt Sally:

'Good gracious! Anybody hurt?'
'No'm. Killed a nigger.'
'Well, it's lucky, because sometimes people do get hurt.' (Ch.32)

Huck has never met Aunt Sally prior to this scene, and in spinning a lie which this stranger will find unobjectionable he correctly assumes that the common notion of Negro subhumanity will be appropriate.

Huck's off-hand remark is intended to exploit Aunt Sally's attitudes, not to express Huck's own. A nigger, Aunt Sally confirms, is not a person. Yet this exchange is hilarious, precisely because we know that Huck is playing upon her glib and conventional bigotry. We know that Huck's relationship to Jim has already invalidated for him such obtuse racial notions. The conception of the 'nigger' is a socially constituted and sanctioned fiction, and it is just as false and as absurd as Huck's explicit fabrication, which Aunt Sally also swallows whole,

In fact, the exchange between Huck and Aunt Sally reveals a great deal about how racial discourse operates. Its function is to promulgate a conception of 'the Negro' as a subhuman and expendable creature, who is by definition feeble-minded, immoral, lazy, and superstitious. One crucial purpose of this social fiction is to justify the abuse and exploitation of Afro-American people by substituting the essentialist fiction of 'Negro-ism' for the actual character of individual Afro-Americans. Hence, in racial discourse every Afro-American becomes just another instance of 'the Negro' – just another 'nigger.' Twain recognises this invidious tendency of race-thinking, however, and he takes every opportunity to expose the mismatch between racial abstractions and real human beings. □

The context Smith supplies is invaluable, though one may have qualifications of his reading of *Huckleberry Finn*. Is it so certain, for example, that Huck is consciously playing on Aunt Sally's 'glib and conventional bigotry' with his remark, 'No'm. Killed a nigger'? Might not the observation be an example of his unconscious, habitual racism? As for the term 'nigger', it is the subject of Smith's further debate:

■ A reader who objects to the word 'nigger' might still insist that Twain could have avoided using it. But it is difficult to imagine how Twain could have debunked a discourse without using the specific terms of that discourse. Even when Twain was writing his book, 'nigger' was universally recognized as an insulting, demeaning word. According to Stuart Berg Flexner, 'Negro' was generally pronounced as 'nigger' until about 1825, at which time Abolitionists began objecting to that term.[24] They preferred 'colored person' or 'person of color.' Hence, W.E.B. Du Bois reports that some black Abolitionists of the early 1830s declared themselves united 'as men, . . . not as slaves'; as 'people of color,' not as 'Negroes'.[25] Writing a generation later in *Army Life in a Black Regiment* (1869), Thomas Wentworth Higginson deplored the common use of 'nigger' among freedmen, which he regarded as evidence of low self-esteem.[26] The objections to 'nigger,' then, are not a consequence of the modern sensibility but had been common for a half-century before *Huckleberry Finn* was published. The specific function of this term in the book, however, is neither to offend nor merely to provide linguistic authenticity. Much more importantly, it establishes a context against which Jim's specific virtues may emerge as explicit refutations of racist presuppositions. ☐

Smith then turns to another recurrent problem:

■ One aspect of *Huckleberry Finn* which has elicited copious critical commentary is Twain's use of superstition. In nineteenth-century racial discourse, 'the Negro' was always defined as inherently superstitious. . . . Many critics, therefore, have cited Jim's superstitious behaviour as an instance of negative stereotyping. One cannot deny that in this respect Jim closely resembles the entire tradition of comic darkies but to observe this similarity is a negligible feat. The issue is, does Twain merely reiterate clichés, or does he use these conventional patterns to make an unconventional point? A close examination will show that in virtually every instance, Twain uses Jim's superstition to make points which undermine rather than revalidate the dominant racial discourse.

The first incident of this superstitious behaviour occurs in chapter 2, as a result of one of Tom Sawyer's pranks. When Jim falls asleep under a tree, Tom hangs his hat on a branch. Subsequently, Jim concocts an elaborate tale about having been hexed and ridden by witches. The tale grows more grandiose with subsequent retellings, and eventually Jim becomes a local celebrity, sporting a five-cent piece on a string around his neck as a talisman. 'Niggers would come miles to hear Jim tell about it, and he was more looked up to than any nigger in that country;' the narrator reports. Jim's celebrity finally reaches the point that 'Jim was most ruined, for a servant, because he got so stuck up on account of having seen the devil and been rode by witches.' This is, no doubt, amusing. Yet whether Jim believes his own tale or not – and the 'superstitious Negro' thesis requires us to assume that he does – the fact remains that Jim clearly benefits from becoming more a celebrity and less a 'servant.' It is his owner, not Jim, who suffers when Jim's uncompensated labour diminishes.

This incident has often been interpreted as an example of risible Negro gullibility and ignorance, as exemplified by blackface minstrelsy. Such a reading has more than a little validity; but can only partially account for the implications of this scene. If not for the final sentence, such an account might seem wholly satisfactory; but the information that Jim becomes, through his own storytelling, unsuited for life as a slave, introduces unexpected complications. Is it likely that Jim has been deceived by his own creative prevarications – especially given what we learn about his character subsequently? Or has he cleverly exploited the conventions of 'Negro superstition' in order to turn a silly boy's prank to his own advantage?

Regardless of whether we credit Jim with forethought in this matter, it is undeniable that he turns Tom's attempt to humiliate him into a major personal triumph. In other words, Tom gives him an inch, and he takes an ell. It is also obvious that he does so by exercising remarkable skills as a rhetorician. By constructing a fictitious narrative of his own experience, Jim elevates himself above his prescribed station in life. By becoming, in effect, an author, Jim writes himself a new destiny. Jim's triumph may appear to be dependent upon the gullibility of other 'superstitious' Negroes, but since we have no direct encounter with them, we cannot know whether they are unwitting victims of Jim's ruse or not. A willing audience need not be a totally credulous one. In any case, it is intelligence, not stupidity, which facilitates Jim's triumph. Tom may have had his chuckle, but the last laugh, clearly, belongs to Jim.

In assessing Jim's character, we should keep in mind that forethought, creativity and shrewdness are qualities which racial discourse – see Thomas Jefferson – denies to 'the Negro'. In that sense, Jim's darky performance here subverts the fundamental definition of the darky. For 'the Negro' is defined to be an object, not a subject. Yet does an object construct its own narrative? Viewed in this way, the fact of superstition which traditionally connotes ignorance and unsophistication becomes far less important than the ends to which superstition is put. This inference exposes, once again, the inadequacy of a positivist epistemology, which holds, for example, that a rose is a rose is a rose. No one will deny the self-evidence of a tautology; but a rose derives whatever meaning it has from the context within which it is placed (including the context of traditional symbolism). It is the contextualising activity, not *das Ding-an-sich*, which generates meaning. Again and again, Twain attacks racial essentialism by directing our attention, instead, to the particularity of individual action. We find that Jim is not 'the Negro.' Jim is Jim, and we, like Huck, come to understand what Jim is by attending to what he does in specific situations.

Throughout the novel, Twain presents Jim in ways which render ludicrous the conventional wisdom about 'Negro character'. As an intelligent, sensitive, wily and considerate individual, Jim demonstrates that one's race provides no useful index of one's character. While that point may seem obvious to many contemporary readers, it is a point rarely made by nineteenth-century Euro-American novelists. Indeed, except for Melville, J.W. DeForest, Albion Tourgee, and George Washington Cable, white novelists virtually always portrayed Afro-American characters as exemplifications of 'Negroness.' In this regard, the twentieth century has been little better. By presenting us a series of glimpses which penetrate the 'Negro' exterior and reveal the person beneath it, Twain debunks American racial discourse. For racial discourse maintains that the 'Negro' exterior is all that a 'Negro' really has. □

Granting everything Smith says here, it is also the case that Jim's superstition needs to be related to all the other ways (mainly Christian) in the novel with which characters deal with mystery and the metaphysical. Why are Jim's beliefs more inherently ridiculous, if they are ridiculous at all, than theirs? The Widow Douglas can 'talk about Providence in a way to make a body's mouth water' (Ch.3), but *Huckleberry Finn* is also gladdened by the vitality of Jim's beliefs. Forgetting that the very root of comedy has a natural twist, readers are becoming too nervous and squeamish about the comedy associated with Jim. What Twain is offering in the marvellous inventiveness of Jim's dream in chapter 2 and the fortune telling in chapter 4 is a comedy of wonder at human resourcefulness, when faced with mysteries over which Jim has no more mastery than the rest of us. It is like the self-delight Shakespeare takes in Bottom's dream in *A Midsummer Night's Dream*.

Smith acknowledges some racism in Twain when he recognises that readings which see Jim's dream 'as an example of risible Negro gullibility and ignorance, as exemplified by blackface minstrelsy' have 'more than a little validity'. Hutchinson too returns to this issue in his argument that there is conscious and unconscious racism in *Huckleberry Finn*. The former is the racism Twain is aware of. He exhibits it in Huck, so that readers may be more enlightened than Huck. Learning that Jim intends to steal his wife and children from their slave-owner, they may not be as appalled as Huck. The unconscious racism, in Hutchinson's view, belongs to both Huck and Twain, because Twain himself is unaware of it. It is presented straight, without any invitation to criticism, and culminates in Huck's final praise for Jim: 'I knowed he was white inside.' 'Who', Hutchinson asks,

■ . . . would not be happier if *Huckleberry Finn* did not contain such a line? Yet great books are not written from within the stockade of unblemished moral positions. Consciously and unconsciously, they participate in the corruptions they address. In Yeats' words from 'The Circus Animals' Desertion', they begin 'In the foul rag-and-bone shop of the heart'. □

Is such a defence of the racism in *Huckleberry Finn*, recognising as it does the historical context of the work, sufficient? Presumably not for readers like Wallace, who are personally and deeply offended. Why should they consent to humiliation, so that great writing may happen? It may indeed be the case that not even the greatest works of art can always resolve every conflict that might exist between them and every potential audience. Yet we also want art to push at the boundaries of our sense of reality and morality, and to transform our certainties, otherwise why bother with it? In his plays Shakespeare habitually finds murderers more interesting than he might if he were about to become an immediate victim in real life. *The Merchant of Venice* and *Othello* are also replete with racism and in this respect shed useful light on *Huckleberry Finn*. I would argue they are plays about racism rather than racist plays, but it is their formal contrast with Twain's novel that is most illuminating. Whatever racism is in either play is completely objectified. It belongs to the character who voices it and is heard by audiences or read by readers without mediation from an author or a narrator. Seemingly, characters express prejudice, as they express everything else, independently of Shakespeare, making it impossible to get back to whatever views he actually held. Pap is similarly objectified in his diatribe about the 'free nigger' in chapter 6. He exemplifies racist paranoia, recorded with fascination by Twain through an invisible Huck. Arguably, the variety of scenes involving Huck and Jim ought also to be seen as objective, as if we are engaging with several possibilities of relationship between an inherently prejudiced white boy and escaping adult black slave. The identity either character adopts at any one time is mutually determined, so that the final escapades at the Phelps' are an objective version of what a white imagination might turn a black man into. Unfortunately, the form of *Huckleberry Finn* cannot consistently accomplish this kind of objectivity. It has a narrator who provides our only access to what happens. What he says, or does not say, counts. If he goes along with Jim being treated like a simpleton, it is tempting to feel the novel itself endorses this treatment. If we succumb to this temptation, the scenes at the Phelps' are not an exhibition by Twain of how the empowered white imagination (even when belonging to mere boys) may transform a black man; rather they display qualities of compliant and simple gullibility in Jim which Twain himself can believe are inherent in his blackness.

Our final critic, Shelley Fisher Fishkin,[27] attempts fundamentally to re-position *Huckleberry Finn*. It is appropriate to conclude with her, since she finds the thrust for her thesis in the writings of Ellison and Morrison, the last of the creative writers already referred to. Like Ellison, Morrison[28] is countering the assumption that 'traditional, canonical American literature is free of, uninformed, and unshaped by the four-hundred-year-old presence of, first, Africans and then African–Americans in the United States'. Responding to this necessary corrective, Fishkin takes a large step. Knowing that Twain claimed he based Huck Finn on Tom Blankenship, the poor white son of the town drunkard,[29] Fishkin claims:

■ Compelling evidence indicates that the model for Huck Finn's voice was a black child instead of a white one and that this child's speech sparked in Twain a sense of the possibilities of a vernacular narrator. The record suggests that it may have been yet another black speaker who awakened Twain to the power of satire as a tool of social criticism. (p.4) □

The 'compelling evidence' Fishkin produces is Twain's article 'Sociable Jimmy'.[30] This records his being entertained in his hotel room, on a public lecture tour, by a 'bright, simple, guileless little darkey boy'. In fact the evidence is anything but convincing for Fishkin's case. Not only does it lack any verification other than her insistence, but also the voice from *Huckleberry Finn* that Jimmy's most anticipates is Jim's. It is all the more odd, therefore, that Fishkin should conclude that in *Huckleberry Finn* itself 'Jim's voice is, ultimately, a diminished voice, a voice cramped within boundaries as confining as his prison-shack on the Phelps Plantation' (p.107). Nor is she more successful in demonstrating her second claim. To argue that Twain's power of satire and his awareness of 'intertextuality and . . . attention to the gaps between "surface" and meaning' should be awakened by another single black source (pp.53–5) is to write off an immense amount of readily available English satirical literature, not to mention the Southwestern humorists of whom Fishkin is fully aware.

But is Huck black in the sense that he is not just white? Is he female in the sense that he is not just male? Like all great works of literature *Huckleberry Finn* engages universally with reader and audience imagination. This effect is apparent when Fishkin, who is full of rewarding incidentals, is debating racial stereotyping (pp.88–9) in *Huckleberry Finn*. Acknowledging that Twain may have subverted such stereotypes in the novel, she points out that

■ . . . he made no effort to prevent his text from being presented to the public in ways that emphasised its connection to familiar minstrel-show traditions, and indeed, often participated in this process himself. For example, although he complained to illustrator Edward W. Kemble that the first pictures of Huck were not 'good-looking' enough, Twain raised no objection to Kemble's drawings of Jim, who (particularly in the early illustrations) looked much like all of Kemble's characteristic 'comically represented Negroes.'[31]

When portions of the novel were excerpted in newspapers would not a piece about 'Jim's Investments' taken out of context suggest a minstrel routine more than anything else? ('Jim's Investments' ran in the 'Passing Pleasantry' column in the *Cleveland Leader*, 11 January 1885, identified as reprinted from *The Century*. It also ran in the *Boston*

Budget on 4 January 1885.) More significantly, some of the passages from the book with which Twain most liked to entertain audiences during readings from the 1880s through the 1890s were passages that strike readers today as most redolent of the minstrel show: 'King Sollermun' and 'Jim's Bank'.

One might argue that the closing sentences of each piece took it beyond the realm of minstrelsy into a subtle or not-so-subtle critique of race slavery. Jim's comment, 'I owns mysef' evokes sober pathos, not ridicule; and by the end of 'King Sollermun,' as David Smith has noted, Jim's argument appears more convincing than Huck's, making Huck's comment that you 'can't learn a nigger to argue' sound clearly like his own 'sour grapes.'[32] The reader – and audience – is more likely to challenge Huck on this pronouncement than to agree with him. We do not have the evidence to prove, however, that Twain's white lecture audiences got these points; it is quite possible they responded to the pieces precisely as minstrel routines. On this point, it is interesting to note, however, that in his readings Twain sometimes preceded 'Jim's Bank' with 'A True Story' and 'Call this a govment,' setting it in a context shaped by Aunt Rachel's powerful sincerity and Pap's self-parodic racism. Twain does not seem to have been particularly concerned about the links that might have been forming in the public's mind between minstrel traditions and aspects of his work.[33] What are we to make of the fact that Twain's readings were in demand among black audiences as well as white? □

What we are to make is that the black audience found it funny. To laugh at oneself, if the black audience was laughing at itself, is as liberating in imagination as any other experience.

CRITICAL WORKS CITED

W.H. Auden, 'Huck and Oliver', *The Listener*, 50, October 1953, pp.540–1.

Millicent Bell, '*Huckleberry Finn:* Journey Without End', *Virginia Quarterly Review*, 58, Spring 1982, pp.252–67.

Arnold Bennett, '[Mark Twain]', *Bookman*, London, 37, June 1910, p.118.

Walter Blair, 'When Was *Huckleberry Finn* Written?', *American Literature*, 30, March 1958, pp.1–25.

Walter Blair, *Mark Twain and Huck Finn*, Berkeley and Los Angeles 1962.

Van Wyck Brooks, *The Ordeal of Mark Twain*, New York 1920; revised 1933.

James M. Cox, 'Remarks on the Sad Initiation of Huckleberry Finn', *Sewanee Review*, 62, July–September 1954, pp.389–405.

James M. Cox, *Mark Twain: The Fate of Humor*, Princeton 1966.

Bernard DeVoto, *Mark Twain's America*, Boston 1932.

Bernard DeVoto, *Mark Twain at Work*, Cambridge, Mass. 1942.

A.E. Dyson, '*Huckleberry Finn* and the Whole Truth', *Critical Quarterly*, 3, Spring 1961, pp.29–40.

T.S. Eliot, 'Introduction' *Huckleberry Finn*, London 1950.

Ralph Ellison, *Shadow and Act*, New York 1964.

Ralph Ellison, 'What America Would Be Like Without Blacks' *Time*, 6 April 1970, reprinted in *Going to the Territory*, New York 1987, pp.104–12.

William Faulkner, in James B. Meriwether and Michael Millgate, eds, *Lion in the Garden: Interviews with William Faulkner, 1926–1962*, New York 1968.

Leslie A. Fiedler, 'Come Back to the Raft Ag'in, Huck Honey!' *Partisan Review*, 15, June 1948, pp.269–76.

Leslie A. Fiedler, *Love and Death in the American Novel*, New York 1960.

Victor Fischer, 'Huck Finn Reviewed: The Reception of *Huckleberry Finn* in the United States, 1885–97', *American Literary Realism: 1870–1910*, 16, Spring 1983, pp.1–57.

Shelley Fisher Fishkin, *Was Huck Black? Mark Twain and African–American Voices*, New York and Oxford 1993.

F. Scott Fitzgerald, *Fitzgerald Newsletter*, No. 8, Winter 1960.

Helen L. Harris, 'Mark Twain's Response to the Native American', *American Literature*, 46, January 1975, pp.495–505.

Ernest Hemingway, *Green Hills of Africa*, New York 1935.

Hamlin L. Hill, 'The Composition and the Structure of *Tom Sawyer*', *American Literature*, 32, January 1961, pp.379–92.

William Dean Howells, *My Mark Twain*, 1, New York and London 1910.

Stuart Hutchinson, *Mark Twain: Humour on the Run*, Amsterdam and Atlanta, GA 1994.

Alexander E. Jones, 'Mark Twain and Sexuality', *PMLA*, 71, September 1956, pp.595–616.

Justin Kaplan, *Mr Clemens and Mark Twain*, New York 1966.

Alfred Kazin, 'Creature of Circumstances: Mark Twain', *An American Procession*, New York 1984, pp.181–210.

Leland Krauth, 'Mark Twain: The Victorian of Southwestern Humor', *American Literature*, 54, October 1982, pp.368–84.

D.H. Lawrence, 'Max Havelaar, by E.D. Decker (Multatuli, pseud.)', in Edward

D. McDonald, ed., *Phoenix: The Posthumous Papers of D.H. Lawrence*, London and New York 1936, pp.236–9.

Norman Mailer, 'Huck Finn, Alive at 100', *The New York Times Book Review*, 89, 9 December 1984, pp.1, 36–7.

Dwight MacDonald, 'Mark Twain: An Unsentimental Journey', *The New Yorker*, 36, 9 April 1960, pp.160–96; repr. in *Against the American Grain*, New York 1962, pp.80–122.

Leo Marx, 'Mr Eliot, Mr Trilling and Huckleberry Finn', *The American Scholar*, 22, Autumn 1953, pp.423–40.

Toni Morrison, *Playing in the Dark: Whiteness and the Literary Imagination*, Cambridge, Mass. 1992.

Arthur G. Pettit, 'Mark Twain's Attitude Toward the Negro in the West, 1861–67', *The Western Historical Quarterly*, 1, January 1970, pp.51–62.

Arthur G. Pettit, 'Mark Twain and the Negro', *Journal of Negro History*, 56, April 1971, pp.88–96.

V.S. Pritchett, 'Books in General', *New Statesman and Nation*, 113, 2 August 1941, pp.113.

Philip Rahv, 'The Cult of Experience in American Writing', *Image and Idea* 1949; reprinted by Greenwood Press, Westport, Connecticut 1978.

Charlie Reilly, 'An Interview with John Barth', *Contemporary Literature*, 22, Winter 1981, pp.1–23.

David L. Smith, 'Huck, Jim, and American Racial Discourse', *Mark Twain Journal*, 22, 1984, pp.4–12.

Henry Nash Smith, 'Introduction', *Adventures of Huckleberry Finn*, Cambridge, Mass. 1958, pp.v–xix.

Tom H. Towers, 'I Never Thought We Might Want to Come Back: Strategies of Transcendence in Tom Sawyer', *Modern Fiction Studies*, 21, Winter 1975, pp.509–20.

Lionel Trilling, 'Introduction', *The Adventures of Huckleberry Finn*, New York 1948.

Arlin Turner, 'Mark Twain and the South: An Affair of Love and Anger', *The Southern Review*, 4, April 1968, pp.493–519.

Booker T. Washington '[Tributes to Mark Twain]', *North American Review*, 191, June 1910, pp.828–30.

John H. Wallace, 'Huckleberry Finn is Offensive', *Washington Post*, 11 April 1982.

Cynthia Griffin Wolff, 'The Adventures of Tom Sawyer: A Nightmare Vision of American Boyhood', *The Massachusetts Review*, 21, Winter 1980, pp.637–52.

The indispensable bibliography of works on Mark Twain is Thomas Asa Tenney, *Mark Twain: A Reference Guide*, Boston 1977. It contains 4700 entries up to 1974. Thereafter it is kept up to date in an annual supplement in *American Literary Realism: 1870–1910*.

Stuart Hutchinson, ed., *Mark Twain: Critical Assessments*, 4 vols., Helm Information 1993 offers a representative selection of writing on Twain from 1869 to 1992.

NOTES

CHAPTER ONE

1 *Athenaeum*, 24 June 1876, p.851.
2 *Atlantic Monthly*, 37, May 1876, pp.621–2.
3 Justin Kaplan, *Mr Clemens and Mark Twain*, New York, 1966, p.363.
4 *New York Times*, 13 January 1877, p.3.

CHAPTER TWO

1 Hamlin L. Hill, 'The Composition and the Structure of *Tom Sawyer*', *American Literature*, 32, January 1961, pp.379–92.
2 Walter Blair, 'On the Structure of *Tom Sawyer*', *Modern Philology*, 37, August 1939, pp.75–88.
3 Delancey Ferguson, *Mark Twain: Man and Legend*, Indianapolis 1943, p.176.
4 See Bernard DeVoto, *Mark Twain at Work*, Cambridge, Mass. 1942, pp.3–9.
5 Albert B. Paine, *Mark Twain's Letters*, New York 1917, p.224.
6 *Mark Twain's Letters*, p.258.
7 Bernard DeVoto, *Mark Twain in Eruption*, New York 1940, p.197.
8 Brander Matthews, *The Tocsin of Revolt and Other Essays*, New York 1922, p.265.
9 DeVoto (*Mark Twain at Work*, p.6) mentions only one of these many marginal notations, the one on the first page of the manuscript: 'Put in things from Boy – lecture'. The reference was probably to a lecture Twain proposed for the 1871–72 lecture season. In the *American Publisher*, a magazine published by the American Publishing Company, Twain's publisher, and edited by Orion Clemens, Twain's brother, Orion revealed, 'We have the pleasure to announce that Mark Twain will lecture in New England during the ensuing fall, and later, in the Western States. The subject is not yet decided upon. He has two new lectures, one an appeal in behalf of Boy's Rights, and one entitled simply 'D.L.H.' (*American Publisher*, 1, 4 July 1871).
10 On at least one occasion, however, Twain wrote some separate notes relating to his book. In the Aldis Collection of the Yale University Library there is a single page of notes for the graveyard scene:

Potter & Dr
objects to job quarrell [*sic*] fight
Potter knocked down with Tom's shovel
Joe rushed in and stabs Dr Potter insensible
Joe will bury Dr in Tom's hole & will make Potter think he is accessory
Finds treasure – goes and hides it – returns and finds P up
No use to bury body, for Potter thinks he did it
When boys leave, they carry their tools with them & will never tell
Somewhere previously it is said Joe lives in the cave

Since Injun Joe has been substituted for Pap Finn (who originally played this part in the manuscript (see *Mark Twain at Work*, p.17) and since the graveyard and the treasure scenes have been combined, this was probably a note for a lecture or a dramatisation.
11 See *Mark Twain at Work*, p.49 and Albert B. Paine, ed., *Mark Twain's Notebook*, New York 1935, p.212.
12 *Mark Twain's Letters*, pp.258–9. See also his letter to Howells of 21 June 1875 in *Mark Twain at Work*, p.10, n.2.
13 4 September 1874, *Mark Twain's Letters*, p.234.
14 *Mark Twain in Eruption*, p.197.
15 Court trials with surprise witnesses and sensational evidence were the ingredients of one of Mark Twain's favourite plots. They occurred in 'At Sin', 'Simon Wheeler, the Amateur Detective', and several of the trials analysed in D.M. McKeithan, *Court Trials in Mark Twain and Other Essays*, The Hague 1958, pp.10–114.
16 *Mark Twain's Letters*, p.259.
17 The first three pages of the picnic material were originally numbered '535' to '537'. The next eight pages were '338' to '345'. The two-hundred-page drop in pagination was apparently inadvertent. There is no indication in the manuscript that this material might have belonged at page 338. Twain was making preparations for the picnic in Chapter XVII, 145,

pp.87–90.

18 *The Tocsin of Revolt and Other Essays*, p.266.

19 'On the Structure of *Tom Sawyer*', p.87. 'And well in the second half of the book, in a series of chapters – XX, XXIII, XXXII – come those crucial situations in which he acts more like a grownup than like an irresponsible boy.'

20 'On the Structure of *Tom Sawyer*', p.85.

21 Bernard DeVoto, *Mark Twain at Work*, Cambridge, Mass. 1942, pp.3–24.

22 Dwight MacDonald, 'Mark Twain: An Unsentimental Journey', *The New Yorker*, 36, 9 April 1960, pp.160–96; reprinted in *Against the American Grain*, New York 1962, pp.80–122.

23 Alfred Kazin, 'Creature of Circumstances: Mark Twain', *An American Procession*, New York 1984, pp.181–210.

24 Hamlin Hill, 'Mark Twain and the American Publishing Company' (unpublished doctoral dissertation, University of Chicago 1949).

25 A.M. Broadley, *Chats on Autographs*, New York 1910, p.229. Paine, who thought his version of the remark too racy for anything but the small print of a footnote, erroneously assigned it to the first meeting of the pair.

26 Mildred Howells, ed., *Life in Letters of William Dean Howells*, Garden City 1923, 1, p.212.

27 *Mark Twain at Work*, pp.10–14, remarks all the changes reported here.

28 Walter Blair, *Mark Twain and Huck Finn*, Berkeley and Los Angeles 1962, pp.78–81.

29 James M. Cox, 'Remarks on the Sad Initiation of Huckleberry Finn', *Sewanee Review*, 62, July–September 1954, pp.389–405.

30 Tom H. Towers, 'I Never Thought We Might Want to Come Back: Strategies of Transcendence in *Tom Sawyer*', *Modern Fiction Studies*, 21, Winter 1975, pp.509–20.

31 Arthur G. Pettit, 'Mark Twain's Attitude Toward the Negro in the West, 1861–67' (*The Western Historical Quarterly*, 1, January 1970, pp.51–62.

32 Arthur G. Pettit, 'Mark Twain and the Negro' (*Journal of Negro History*, 56, April 1971, pp.88–96)

33 Arlin Turner, 'Mark Twain and the South: An Affair of Love and Anger', *The Southern Review*, 4, April 1968, 493–519.

34 Helen L. Harris, 'Mark Twain's Response to the Native American', *American Literature*, 46, Jan 1975, pp.495–505.

35 Cynthia Griffin Wolff, '*The Adventures of Tom Sawyer:* A Nightmare Vision of American Boyhood', *The Massachusetts Review*, 21, Winter 1980, pp.637–52.

36 Stuart Hutchinson, *Mark Twain: Humour on the Run*, Amsterdam, Atlanta 1994, pp.45–63.

37 Howells' early impression of Livy was that she was 'the very flower and perfume of Ladylikeness' (*Life in Letters*, 1, p.187).

38 Van Wyck Brooks (*The Ordeal of Mark Twain*, New York 1920, p.183) interprets Twain's desire to show himself off and his love of the limelight as an example of Adler's 'masculine protest'.

39 Albert Bigelow Paine, *Mark Twain: A Biography*, New York 1912, 1, p.524. See also Howells, *My Mark Twain*, New York, London 1910, pp.4–5.

40 *The Ordeal of Mark Twain*, p.183.

41 J.F. Brown, *The Psychodynamics of Abnormal Behaviour*, New York 1940, p.159.

42 Albert Bigelow Paine, ed., *Mark Twain's Notebook*, New York 1935, pp.387. In keeping with his masochistic temperament, Twain was not only reproaching himself for mistreating Livy but was simultaneously feeling neglected: 'and there . . . she lay white and cold and unresponsive to my reverent caresses – a new thing to me and a new thing to her, that had not happened before in five and thirty years' (Albert Bigelow Paine, ed., *Mark Twain's Letters*, New York 1917, 2, p.761). Yet there is something very curious about her last years. While she was ill in Italy, almost everyone could visit her except her husband – who was limited to occasional visits of a few minutes' duration.

43 Alexander E. Jones, 'Mark Twain and

Sexuality', *PMLA*, 71, September 1956, pp.595–616.

CHAPTER THREE

1 Walter Blair, 'When Was Huckleberry Finn Written?', *American Literature*, 30, March 1958, pp.1–25.

2 *Mark Twain's Letters*, 1, pp.282–3.

3 *Mark Twain's Letters*, 1, p.436 and W.B. Gates, ed., 'Mark Twain to His English Publishers', *American Literature*, 11, March 1939, p.79.

4 Walter Blair, *Mark Twain and Huck Finn*, Berkeley and Los Angeles 1962, pp.103, 151.

5 Victor Fischer, 'Huck Finn Reviewed: The Reception of Huckleberry Finn in the United States, 1885–97', *American Literary Realism: 1870–1910*, 16, Spring 1983, pp.1–57).

6 *Harper's Monthly*, 93, September 1896; Advertiser, p.3.

7 Boston *Transcript*, 17 March 1885, p.4; reprinted in Kenneth S. Lynn, *Huckleberry Finn: Text, Sources, Criticism*, New York 1961, p.171. Concord librarian was Ellen F. Whitney. Three of the more prominent men of the Concord Library Committee were: Edward Waldo Emerson, son of Ralph Waldo, an instructor at the Museum of Fine Arts in Boston in 1885; George Augustus King, lawyer and former state senator; James Lyman Whitney, librarian at the Boston Library, and chairman of the School Committee of Concord. Albert Tolman was secretary of the Library Committee. I thank Marcia E. Moss of the Concord Public Library for her help in uncovering information about membership of the 1885 Library Committee.

8 St Louis *Globe Democrat*, 17 March 1885, p.1.

9 New York *Herald*, 18 March 1885, p.6.

10 San Jose *Times–Mercury*, 18 March 1885, p.4.

11 Stockton *Evening Mail*, 19 March 1885, p.2.

12 Boston *Daily Globe*, 17 March 1885, p.2

13 New York *World*, 18 March 1885, p.4.

14 St Louis *Post–Dispatch*, 17 March 1885, p.4

15 Hartford *Courant*, 18 March 1885, p.2

16 New York *Sun*, 18 March 1885, p.2.

17 Concord *Freeman*, 20 March 1885, n.p.

18 Clemens to Webster, 18 March 1885. This now famous letter has been printed or quoted in a number of places; for the full text see *Mark Twain's Letters*, 2, pp.452–3.

19 For accounts of the readings see Paul Fatout, *Mark Twain on the Lecture Circuit*, Bloomington 1960, pp.214–29, and Guy A. Cardwell, *Twins of Genius*, Michigan State College Press 1953. In addition, Paul Fatout has generously left on deposit in the Mark Twain Papers a large collection of photocopies of contemporary newspaper accounts of the tour. For a list of contemporary interviews, see Louis J. Budd, 'A Listing of and Selection from Newspaper and Magazine Interviews with Samuel L. Clemens, 1874–1910', *American Literary Realism*, 10, Winter 1977, pp.3–5.

20 For an account of the syndication see *Adventures of Huckleberry Finn*, ed. Walter Blair and Victor Fischer, Berkeley Los Angeles London 1984.

21 For quotations from the *World* story and citations to others see Arthur Lawrence Vogelback, 'The Publication and Reception of Huckleberry Finn in America', *American Literature*, 11, November 1939, pp.262–3. Merle Johnson, *A Bibliography of the Works of Mark Twain*, rev. ed. New York 1935, pp.47–9 and Walter Blair, *Mark Twain and Huck Finn*, pp.364–7, give accounts of the discovery and subsequent flurry when the publisher demanded return of the mutilated page from the distributed prospectuses, and the printer was forced to replace the page in 'thousands' of already printed volumes.

22 Walter Blair, *Mark Twain and Huck Finn*, p.366.

23 Andrew Lang, *London Illustrated News*, 98, 14 February 1891, p.222; reprinted in

Critic, 18, 7 March 1891, *Critic*, 19, 25 July 1891, and Frederick Anderson, ed., *Mark Twain: The Critical Heritage*, New York 1971, pp.131–5.

24 Brander Matthews, *Cosmopolitan*, 12, March 1892, pp.636–40.

25 *Punch*, 4 January 1896, pp.4–5.

26 *Outlook*, 53, 13 June 1896, 1115. No later assessment of Mark Twain in *The Outlook* has been found.

27 *Nation*, 62, 11 June 1896, p.454.

28 *Critic*, 28, 20 June 1896, p.446.

29 Chicago *Dial*, 21, 1 July 1896, p.24.

30 *Independent*, 48, 23 July 1896, p.19.

31 *Harper's Monthly*, 93, September 1896, Advertiser, p.3.

32 *Harper's Monthly*, 93, September 1896, Literary Notes, p.2.

33 Brander Matthews, *Book Buyer*, n.s.13, January 1897, pp.978–9.

34 *Athenaeum*, No. 2983, 27 December 1884, p.855.

35 James M. Cox, *Mark Twain: The Fate of Humor*, Princeton 1966.

36 *Saturday Review*, 54, 31 January 1885, pp.153–4.

37 *Saturday Review*, 49, 7 March 1885, pp.301–2.

38 *Century Magazine* 30, May 1885, pp.171–2.

CHAPTER FOUR

1 *London Bookman*, 37, June 1910, p.118.

2 T.S. Eliot, Introduction, *Huckleberry Finn*, London 1950.

3 Edward D. McDonald, ed., *Phoenix: The Posthumous Papers of D.H. Lawrence*, London 1936, pp.236–9.

4 Van Wyck Brooks, *The Ordeal of Mark Twain*, New York 1920; revised 1933.

5 Bernard DeVoto, *Mark Twain's America*, Boston 1932.

6 W.H. Auden, 'Huck and Oliver', *The Listener*, 50, October 1953, pp.540–1.

7 V.S. Pritchett, 'Books in General', *New Statesman and Nation*, 113, 2 August 1941, p.113.

8 *Fitzgerald Newsletter*, No. 8, Winter 1960.

9 William Dean Howells, *My Mark Twain: Reminiscences and Criticisms*, 2, New York and London 1910, ch.11.

10 Justin Kaplan, *Mr Clemens and Mark Twain*, New York 1946, p.46.

11 Hemingway, *Green Hills of Africa*, New York 1935, pp.22–3.

12 *Image and Idea*, 1949, reprinted Greenwood Press, Westport Connecticut 1978, pp.6–21.

13 James B. Meriwether and Michael Millgate, eds., *Lion in the Garden: Interviews with William Faulkner, 1926–1962*, New York 1968, p.65.

14 Meriwether and Millgate (1968), p.137.

15 'Huck Finn, Alive at 100', *The New York Times Book Review*, 89, 9 December 1984, pp.1, 36–7.

16 Charlie Reilly, 'An Interview with John Barth', *Contemporary Literature*, 22, Winter 1981, pp.1–23.

17 *North American Review*, 191, June 1910, pp.828–30.

18 *The Norton Anthology of American Literature*, fourth edition, 2, New York 1994, p.604.

19 Both reprinted in *Shadow and Act*, New York 1964, pp.24–44, 45–59.

20 Leslie Fiedler, Introduction, *Love and Death in the American Novel*, New York 1960.

21 *Time*, 6 April 1970, reprinted in *Going to the Territory*, New York 1987, pp.104–12.

22 Toni Morrison, *Playing in the Dark: Whiteness and the Literary Imagination*, Cambridge, Mass. 1992.

CHAPTER FIVE

1 *Partisan Review*, 15, June 1948, pp.269–76.

2 Lionel Trilling, Introduction to *The Adventures of Huckleberry Finn*, New York 1948.

3 In Joyce's *Finnegans Wake* both Mark Twain and Huckleberry Finn appear frequently. The theme of rivers is, of course, dominant in the book; and Huck's name suits Joyce's purpose, as so many names do, for Finn is one of the many names of his hero. Mark Twain's love of and gift for the spoken language makes another reason for Joyce's interest in him.

4 Leo Marx, 'Mr Eliot, Mr Trilling and Huckleberry Finn', *The American Scholar*, 22, Autumn 1953, pp.423–4.

5 James M. Cox, 'Remarks on the Sad Initiation of Huckleberry Finn', *Sewanee Review*, 62, July–September 1954, pp.389–405.

6 Henry Nash Smith, 'Introduction', *Adventures of Huckleberry Finn*, Cambridge, Mass. 1958, pp.v–xix.

7 It is not clear how thoroughly Clemens had understood the legal status of runaway slaves in Illinois when he was a boy, or what he remembered about this complex subject when he wrote *Huckleberry Finn*. But everyone in Hannibal must have been generally familiar with the state of affairs just across the River. In the 1840s Cairo, in southern Illinois, was rather less safe for a runaway slave than would have been the Illinois shore just opposite Hannibal. To be sure, the farther the fugitive travelled in any direction the harder it was for agents sent out by his owner to overtake him. But in the 1840s a system of 'indentured labour' hardly distinguishable from slavery was in full legal force in Illinois, and the laws of the state directed county officials to arrest any Negro who could not show freedom papers signed by his former master. Generally speaking, pro-slavery sentiment and the eagerness of sheriffs to capture runaway slaves increased as one moved southward in the state (Norman D. Harris, *History of Negro Slavery in Illinois and of the Slavery Agitation in That State*, Chicago 1906, pp.22–3, 53, 109–10). Jim seems to have been familiar with the status of Negroes in Illinois, for in calmer moments he and Huck had wisely planned to go far up the Ohio River by steamboat, perhaps as far as the state of Ohio, where they might have established contact with the Underground Railway. With this sort of help they would have had a good chance to reach Canada, in the manner of Eliza and George Harris in *Uncle Tom's Cabin*. Only in Canada would Jim be immune from arrest and delivery back to his mistress.

8 A.E. Dyson, 'Huckleberry Finn and the Whole Truth', *Critical Quarterly*, 3, Spring 1961, pp.29–40.

9 Millicent Bell, 'Huckleberry Finn: Journey Without End', *Virginia Quarterly Review*, 58, Spring 1982, pp.252–67.

10 Leland Krauth, 'Mark Twain: The Victorian of Southwestern Humor', *American Literature*, 54, October 1982, pp.3, 8–84.

11 Hennig Cohen, 'Mark Twain's Sut Lovingood', in Ben Harris McClary, ed., *The Lovingood Papers*, Knoxville 1962, p.21.

12 Hamlin Hill. *Mark Twain: God's Fool*, New York 1973, p.269.

13 Theodore Hornburger, ed., *Mark Twain's Letters to Will Bowen*, Austin 1941, pp.13–14.

14 Louise K. Barnett, 'Huck Finn: Picaro as Linguistic Outsider', *College Literature*, 6, 1979, p.225.

15 The seminal discussion of the frame device, a hallmark of Southwestern humour, is Walter Blair, *Native American Humor*, New York 1937, pp.90–2. Two useful yet differing perspectives on the humour generated by the frame are provided by Louis J. Budd, 'Gentlemanly humorists of the Old South', *Southern Folklore Quarterly*, 17, 1953, pp.232–40, who emphasises the elite outlook of these humorists, and James M. Cox, 'Humor of the Old Southwest' in Louis D. Rubin Jr., ed., *The Comic Imagination in America*, New Brunswick 1973, pp.101–12. Cox acknowledges their gentility but none the less stresses their 'co-operation' with the vulgar heroes.

16 Stuart Hutchinson, *Mark Twain: Humour on the Run*, Amsterdam, Atlanta 1994, pp.45–63.

17 Arlin Turner, 'Mark Twain and the South: An Affair of Love and Anger', *The Southern Review*, 4, April 1968, pp.493–519.

18 John H. Wallace, 'Huckleberry Finn is Offensive', *Washington Post*, 11 April 1982.

19 David L. Smith, 'Huck, Jim, and American Racial Discourse', *Mark Twain Journal*, 22, 1984, pp.4–12.

20 The literature of the abolition movement and antebellum debates regarding the Negro is, of course, voluminous. George Frederickson's excellent *The Black Image in the White Mind*, New York 1971 is perhaps the best general work of its kind. Frederickson's *The Inner Civil War*, New York 1971 is also valuable, especially pp.53–64. Leon F. Litwack's *North of Slavery*, Chicago 1961, pp.214–46 examines the ambivalence of abolitionists regarding racial intermingling. Benjamin Quarles' *Black Abolitionists*, New York 1969 presents the most detailed examination of black Abolitionists, though Vincent Harding's *There is a River*, New York 1981, pp.101–94 offers a more vivid (and overtly polemical) account of their relationship to white Abolitionists.

21 The debate over Jefferson's relationship to Sally Hemings has raged for two centuries, The most scholarly accounts are by Fawn Brodie (*Thomas Jefferson: An Intimate History*, New York 1974), who suggests that Jefferson did have a prolonged involvement with Hemings, and by Virginius Dabney (*The Jefferson Scandals*, New York 1981), who endeavours to exonerate Jefferson of such charges. Barbara Chase-Riboud presents a fictionalised version of the relationship in *Sally Hemings*, 1979. The first Afro-American novel, *Clotel; Or the President's Daughter*, 1853 by William Wells Brown, was also based on this alleged affair.

22 My use of 'racial discourse' has some affinities to Foucault's conception of 'discourse'. This is not, however, a strictly Foucaultian reading. While Foucault's definition of discursive practice provides one of the most sophisticated tools presently available for cultural analysis, his conception of power seems to me problematic. I prefer an account of power which allows for a consideration of interest and hegemony.

23 This is not to discount the sufferings of other groups. But historically, the philosophical basis of Western racial discourse – which existed even before the European 'discovery' of America – has been the equation of 'good' and 'evil' with light and darkness (or, white and black). . . . Economically, the slave trade, chattel slavery, agricultural peonage, and colour-coded wage differentials have made the exploitation of African–Americans the most profitable form of racism. Finally, Afro-Americans have long been the largest American 'minority' group.

24 Stuart Berg Flexner, *I Hear America Talking*, New York 1976, p.57.

25 William E.B. Du Bois, *The Souls of Black Folk*, in John Hope Franklin, ed., *Three Negro Classics*, New York 1965, p.245.

26 Thomas Wentworth Higginson, *Army Life in a Black Regiment*, Boston 1962, p.28.

27 Shelley Fisher Fishkin, *Was Huck Black? Mark Twain and African–American Voices*, New York, Oxford 1993.

28 Toni Morrison, *Playing in the Dark*, Ch.l.

29 A.B. Paine, ed., *Mark Twain's Autobiography*, 2, New York 1924, pp.174–5.

30 *New York Times*, 29 November 1874.

31 Guy Cardwell, *The Man Who Was Mark Twain: Images and Ideologies*, New Haven 1919, p.196.

32 David Smith, 'Huck, Jim, and American Racial Discourse', *Mark Twain Journal*, 22, Fall 1984, pp.4–12.

33 Arthur J. Berret ('Huckleberry Finn and the Minstrel Show', *American Studies*, 27, 1986, pp.37–49) argues convincingly that 'much of the aesthetic structure of the novel as a whole may have minstrel-show roots'.

ACKNOWLEDGEMENTS

The editor and publishers wish to thank the following for their permission to reprint copyright material: Duke University Press (for material from *American Literature*); Johns Hopkins University Press (for material from *Modern Fiction Studies*); Harvard University Press (for material from *Mark Twain at Work*); Secker & Warburg (for material from *An American Procession*); *The Citadel* (for material from *Mark Twain Journal*); *American Literary Realism*; University of California Press (for material from *Mark Twain and Huck Finn*); *The Massachusetts Review*; Cresset Press (for material from *Huckleberry Finn*); *The New York Times*.

Every effort has been made to contact the holders of any copyrights applying to the material quoted in this book. The publishers would be grateful if any such copyright holders whom they have not been able to contact, would write to them.

Stuart Hutchinson is a Senior Lecturer in English and American Literature at the University of Kent at Canterbury. He has written books on Henry James, Mark Twain and nineteenth century American Literature, and edited essays on Twain and George Eliot. He is especially interested in a comparative approach to English and American literature and is currently writing on George Eliot and Edith Wharton. He is editing the Icon *Critical Guide* to Wharton.

INDEX

PS
1306
M37
1999

Mark Twain.

$39.50

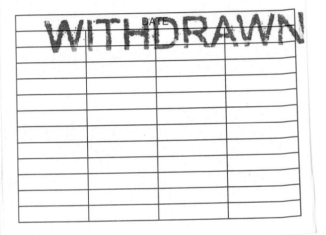